IRONSTRUCK

THE IRONMAN JOURNEY: AN INSPIRATIONAL, COMMON SENSE GUIDE FOR THE NOVICE TRIATHLETE.

IRONSTRUCK

AUTHOR BIOGRAPHY

The author is 57 years old and resides in Calgary, Alberta Canada.

Inspired by the 1976 Olympic games in Montreal, he was driven to take up the sport of distance running, despite being a heavy smoker and most likely the poorest physical condition of his life. After winning the battle against his nicotine addiction, the quest for the distant marathon finish line began. In the beginning it seemed like nothing more than a passing fancy as running just two laps around the inside of gym was physically demanding. Soon however, the two laps became five and then ten and three weeks later a mile. It wasn't long before the more serious running outside began and one mile became five and then ten. In the Spring of 1977 he crossed the finish line of his first marathon in Calgary, Alberta.

Many more marathons and a fifty mile road race were to follow over the following five years and it was 1982 when he witnessed his first Ironman Triathlon and was driven by some unknown force to cross yet another distant finish line. This despite a healthy fear of the water and the inability to swim a single stroke. Most of 1983 was spent learning how to swim from the grass roots level (holding his nose and bobbing under the ever watchful eye of his instructor) and soon he managed his first complete length of the pool (well actually, it was a width.) The length came soon after and one length became ten and than twenty and eventually it grew to two miles in the pool.

In the Fall of 1984, against all odds, he found himself at the starting line of the Hawaii Ironman in Kona along with just over one thousand other daring souls and some fourteen hours later crossed the finish line of what would soon become one of the most challenging and cherished endurance races in the world.

In total fourteen Ironman races were entered and included races in Hawaii, Coeur D'Alene, Idaho and Penticton, B.C. Canada. Ten of the races were in Canada and included a personal best time as an age-grouper of ten hours and forty six minutes. The marathons also continued and included a personal best time of 2 hours 54 minutes. The last Ironman was completed in Idaho in 2004 and the last marathon was run in 2005. In total, the authors' endurance racing career spans a quarter of a century and along with the Ironman races, includes 2--50 mile ultra-marathons, over 30 marathons and also near 100 other road races of varying distances.

As of the writing of this book, the running career still continues and another Ironman one year in the future is not out of the question.

INTRODUCTION

The Ironman Triathlon. The very words conjure up images of a frenetic, heart pounding swim start, muscle searing hill climbs on finely tuned tri-bikes and the unforgiving, relentless marathon. You first saw it on T.V. or went to support a friend or relative in their attempt. Possibly you were a volunteer. Ultimately, you were captivated by the human drama and the courage displayed by the participants. It moved you.

The Ironman has called to you much as it called to me some twenty years ago. The magnetic quality of this event has existed since its early years and shows no signs of letting up as races fill faster and faster every year. It seems a new crop of novice ironmen are appearing at an ever increasing rate.

My purpose here is not to undermine any coach you have or any program you might be on. My hope is that through my Ironman Triathlon experience, I can help you avoid some of the pitfalls I encountered. My credentials were earned on the searing lava fields of the King K. highway during one of the hottest Ironman Triathlons ever recorded, on the endless bike climbs of Ironman Canada and the fast, sweeping downhill curves of Coeur d'alene. My resume is the 14 times I stood in the water waiting for the next Ironman to begin.

When you were first "Ironstruck" your initial thought might have been, "I want to cross that finish line more than anything, but look at me. How can I even consider it? Swim all that way. Bike over 100 miles AND run a marathon. Me! I can't imagine it."

You are overweight, you smoke, you have had 3 kids, you are a couch potato, you drink too much, nobody believes in you anyway, you have no self-confidence and you would probably have no support.

Well, you get the picture.

Which one of those descriptions fits you? Maybe more than one. SO WHAT! There is nothing I mentioned that the human spirit cannot overcome. If you want this bad enough, nothing, and I mean nothing, will stop you from finding yourself standing at the start line of your first Ironman Triathon.

The human body is a miracle, and, I believe, the *first* wonder of the world. It is extraordinary in its ability to adapt to the demands placed upon it.

Consider someone who is totally blind and yet lives alone. How on earth you ask, do they manage? How do they move about the room? Simple. Their body, in all its wonder, has adapted to the situation. They can hear the hum of the refrigerator, the ticking clock or that dripping faucet. Sounds that we ignore are sounds that guide them. Their sense of smell and touch has developed along with their need to sense danger in the form of heat or smoke.

A person relegated to a wheel chair will develop very strong arms, because their body has sensed the need. By the same token their legs will fall victim to atrophy because they are not used.

If you choose a sedentary lifestyle and enjoy your beer and cigarettes, your body will be happy to oblige. It will slow the flow of blood throughout your system and let your heart and lungs work a little harder to keep things on a somewhat even keel. It will also gladly store any excess fat for you until further notice. In essence, your body will adapt to how you choose to live. It may not be healthy, but your body is a slave to your every whim.

That will work to your advantage once you are "Ironstruck."

Just watch the metamorphosis if you simply change the signals to your ever willing to please body. Get off that couch and begin to run a little. Go for a swim. Ride your bike a few miles. Oh, do too much too soon and there could be a small rebellion. "Hey! What's going on? This is new. You never used this muscle before! Stop that!"

Then slowly, as you persist, your sore muscles resign themselves to this new task. Something begins to happen. Your amazing body begins to adapt to this new set of demands. It becomes stronger and toned and your heart and lungs and muscles all work as one to provide the strength and endurance you are demanding of it. YOU are changing. YOU are becoming fitter. YOU are the butterfly emerging from the cocoon of lost dreams, unrealized potential and opportunities lost.

It was an eye-opener when in one of my Ironman races, I read a list of participants and their occupations. A farmer in Japan, a CEO from Wall Street, movie stars, pro athletes, firemen, the military, a police officer from Britain, a housewife and mother from Canada. The list goes on and on.

Since its infancy in Hawaii, the irresistible pull of the Ironman has beckoned people from all walks of life and from every corner of the earth. It calls to them as it has called to you. The same call I heard some twenty years ago. From its inception the Ironman has had this same magnetic quality and shows no signs of change any time soon. The popularity of this incredible event continues to grow at an amazing rate.

Something made you pick up this book. Perhaps you are a coach, a pro triathlete, or an age grouper who has already experienced the challenge of this amazing race. Regardless, you are all welcome. However, I wrote this book in the hopes of creating a common sense information source for those who have been "IRONSTRUCK" and face this ultimate challenge for the first time.

You won't find structured workout plans full of intervals and pool sprints and gear ratios. I will leave the technical jargon to the experts. That is not what Ironstruck is about.

Ironstruck is about inspiration, support, and most of all, hope. Hope for everyone who has one eye on that elusive finish line. It's about living the dream and realizing how amazing you really are and for the first time unleashing your full potential on pretty well every level. Ironstruck is for the dreamers. The ones who, with all their heart, just want to finish.

The Ironman highway is more than a path to the finish line. It is the road to awareness and self-discovery. It is in essence, the new you just waiting to be reborn.

Listen. Can you hear them calling?

The voice of the Iron Gods whispering in the hot Pacific winds that sweep over the shimmering lava fields of the King K. highway.

"Come. Come show us. Come show us what you are made of."

So. Now you have been challenged. Enter. Let Ironstruck be part of this incredible journey to guide you and support you in your quest to become a member of the remarkable family called "Ironman."

*To try is to risk failure. But risk must be taken because the greatest hazard of life is to risk nothing. The person who risks nothing does nothing, has nothing, **is** nothing. He may avoid suffering and sorrow, but he simply cannot learn, feel, change, grow, live, and love.*

-- Leo Buscaglia

CONTENTS

(1) IN THE BEGINNING

I remember with profound clarity the day my Ironman experience began. The day I was "Ironstruck." I was watching my favorite T.V. Show -- Wide World of Sports. It was Fall, 1982. It was then I had my first glimpse, my first experience, of the Ironman Triathlon. Like many of you might be, I was a runner. Triathlon was a foreign word to me.

There was the remarkable swim start. I had never seen anything like it. In my wildest dreams I couldn't imagine a 2.4 mile swim.

Then swimmer after swimmer coming out of the water. They disappear into big tents and change and a steady procession of bikes head out of Kona and onto the highway. I remember the announcer saying, "and now they have 112 miles to bike." "Amazing," I thought. Then another change and back on the road to run a full marathon. It was about here that I thought these people were truly nuts. Just the same, I was in awe and couldn't believe what I was seeing. I couldn't begin to imagine what they were experiencing.

Now the cameras pan back into Kona as the first runners arrive. Until finally it's the first woman. It's Julie Moss and she is obviously in big trouble. Just feet from the finish line she collapses over and over. She is even passed by another woman as she lay there. I can remember willing her to get up. To get across that line. And she does.

From that moment, my life changed forever. I was "Ironstruck." I just knew that one day I had to cross that finish line. It hit me then that there were a few minor obstacles. First I had a deep rooted fear of the water and couldn't swim a stroke. Secondly, I had never been on any sort of "road bike." Actually, I hadn't been on any sort of bike since I was twelve years old.

So there I was in my thirties, taking swimming lessons devised for beginner kids. Just letting go of the side of the pool was a terrifying experience. Slowly as the weeks flew by, my confidence grew and I swam my first length. Well, it was a width. A week later it was a length. That's how I spent the better part of 1983 until in early 1984 my first length was now 2 miles in the pool. My entry for the 1984 Hawaii Ironman Triathlon was in the mail. As a Canadian, I could enter as a foreign contestant in those early days. In two weeks, it was official -- I was in.

I bought myself a new $300 road bike that some company had slapped a triathlon decal on. It was a hunk of steel that weighed just less than a compact car. I was all set. Look out Hawaii, here I come. However, the closer the big day came, the more I doubted my own sanity, but I just tried to push my fears to the back of my mind. Then one day, I was there. Knee deep in the warm Kona waters. It was eerily silent as a priest blessed the event. Somehow, that seemed so appropriate. Twelve hundred athletes and all you could hear were the five media helicopters hovering in the distance. Then the anthem...and the cannon. And so it began, my very first Ironman Triathlon.

(2) WHY THE IRONMAN?

Why do the Ironman Triathlon?

I've lost track of how many times over the years I've been asked why I commit so much of my time to preparing for yet another Ironman.

For a long time I found it difficult to come up with a reasonable response, because often I wasn't sure myself. I think what makes it difficult, is goals change as the years pass and so would the answer to the question.

Once I consciously made the decision to do my first race, there was no turning back and my life took on a new direction. It was easily the most important and life changing decision I have ever made. It touched every single aspect of my life.

At 57 years old I don't plan to do an Ironman every year from this point on. However. I've learned from my long career how important maintaining a healthy lifetstyle is to a person's quality of life.

My plan is to do my next Ironman in my 60th year. There is no confusion "why" any longer when I am asked that question again.

By setting that goal, I realize that I will have to stay fit between now and then. It also means that when that starting gun goes off 4 years from now, I will be going into my 60's in absolute peak condition. Most likely among the fittest 60 year olds in the world. Really not a bad group to be a part of at that stage in one's life. How that particular race turns out really has no bearing on anything. Just making it there is reward in itself.

I strongly believe that how successful or rich a person is doesn't really make a whole lot of difference when a twist of fate strips it all away and makes people from all walks of life materially equal and dependent on their own physical strength, courage, and adaptability in order to survive.

The world is changing, and events like 9-11 and hurricane Katrina are examples of catastrophic events that knew no boundaries and in an instant left individuals with nothing but the ability they possessed within themselves to at least provide a fighting chance to survive.

Of course it doesn't mean everyone has to begin training for the Ironman, one of the most challenging endurance events in the world. However, to meet the unexpected circumstances of an ever changing world, individuals are wise to take care of their physical well being to the best of their ability. At any age, and yes, even as we settle into the retirement years.

Perhaps this explains it best.

Twenty-two years ago, had I found myself in the middle of a lake, 5 miles from shore with no life jacket, I would most likely have drowned in less than a minute. Now it would be an opportunity for a long training swim.

The Ironman has given me that ability and that confidence. I owe this amazing event so much.

(3) A QUIET ENTRANCE

The Hawaii Ironman grew from very humble beginnings. Really not much more than a few friends discussing who was the better athlete--a runner, a biker, or a swimmer.

A suggestion was made that a race be invented that included all three elements. That day, an event was born that would change the landscape of sporting history.

What started as a 2.4 Waikiki rough water swim, a bike race around the island, followed by the Honolulu marathon gave birth to multi-event races that had never before existed.

Even races such as the Eco-challenge originated from that small gathering of friends. Little did they know that the race would one day move to Kona on the big island and explode into prominence in 1982 when ABC television covered the race. Television viewers were enthralled when Julie Moss collapsed in sight of Kona and then again feet from the finish line.

Who would have believed back then that the triathlon would find prominence as an Olympic event that draws athletes from countries around the world.

How could they possible imagine that pros would be racing for huge prize money and that amateurs from every corner of the earth would challenge the Ironman distance, forever changing their lives for the better when they realized their dream of crossing that distant finish line.

The amazing thing is, there seems to be no end in sight. Races are filling in record time year after year as individuals from all walks of life are "Ironstruck" and hear the call of the Iron Gods drawing them to this incredible event.

If you are considering challenging the Ironman for the first time, I sincerely hope you do it. Everyone I know who has reached the Ironman finish line has seen it as a life-altering experience. There are countless race-day stories that are shared by those who have been there.

Some are satisfied to finish one race, but there are also those who return year after year to feel that special Ironman bond that can only be experienced by taking part in the frenetic, sometimes terrifying mass swim start, a long bike ride full of climbs and near- misses and harrowing downhill curves and a marathon that will test the will, spirit and courage of everyone who takes on this challenge.

All this thanks to a few friends who had an idea that turned into one of the world's most amazing sporting events that gives the ordinary person the opportunity to accomplish something very, very special.

(4) OVER 45? 10 REASONS TO GO FOR IT

1) Just preparing for an Ironman by dieting and training could well put you in the best physical condition of your life.

2) By improving yourself, you do a wonderful thing for your family and all those close to you.

3) In the eyes of those same people, you will be a role model, a hero and an inspiration.

4) You will give your life new meaning. As a 14 time Ironman (my last at 55), I guarantee it.

5) You will most likely learn new skills you previously knew nothing about. Just learning how to swim is a huge bonus and could one day save your life or the life of someone important to you.

6) In the course of your training and the race experience itself, you will meet some truly remarkable people.

7) You can combine your Ironman race with a holiday and take the family. Most important of all, they will be there to cheer you on and share in your incredible achievement.

8) For the first time, you will learn what you are truly capable of on a physical, emotional and even spiritual level. You will amaze yourself and be a better person for the total experience.

9) You will discover there are few challenges the human spirit cannot

overcome. You will come to realize that the strength within all of us just has to be given an opportunity to show itself.

10) Finish this race and you will forever have the title "Ironman" in front of your name. That can never be taken away from you, and every time you hear the word, you will be reminded of what a remarkable journey it was, and how taking up the challenge was the best decision of your life.

(5) STRIKING A BALANCE

I truly believe there comes a time in everyone's life when they're faced with an opportunity to do something special for themselves that may require them to be a little selfish. As much as you may love family and friends, the time will come when you choose to put yourself first in order to achieve a goal that can have a profound impact on your life.

To me, I have no doubt that attempting your first Ironman is just such a time. By its very nature, it is demanding and often means spending a lot of time away from family. It can put a strain on your social life as well because ultimately, between work and training and recovering the day is just not long enough.

I believe the wisest way to deal with this is to be open about it from the very beginning. Once you've made your decision to give months and months to preparing for your first race, talk to those nearest to you about your decision. Make sure everyone is aware of just how demanding the preparation will be and how much time it will take out of your life.

There are a lot of things to consider. Your diet will most likely change and may be different from those around you. That means cooking at home will be different and ordering at a restaurant will be different. Going to that party on Saturday night and having a few drinks with friends may not be the wisest thing with a four hour bike ride scheduled for first thing Sunday morning. You will require more sleep. A lot of times training can be very demanding and you may not want to do anything when you get home but relax.

There will also be expenses. Equipment to purchase and entry fees to pay. You will most likely have to use up some of your annual holidays for the race as well.

All these things should be discussed at the very beginning so there are no surprises or hurt feelings halfway through your preparation. The support of those around you is an important ingredient in attempting to reach the Ironman finish line.

On the positive side, reaching your goal could well be one of the high points of your life and will most likely change you for the better. You will be a more confident and self aware person. You will learn what you are truly capable of and will amaze those around you and most likely, even yourself. By growing and improving, everyone in your life will benefit from your success.

Just think. Your fitness level will be amazing and as a result so will your overall health. What family would not want that?

The best idea of all though, is to involve them in your dream. Maybe your partner or kids can bike alongside you one day during that ten mile run. Or maybe bike forty or fifty miles to a favorite picnic spot. You start early in the morning and the family drives out and meets you for a picnic at your destination. Just put your bike on the bike rack and drive back home with them. A great way to share a training day.

Best of all you can bring them to the big race. After cheering you on and witnessing your awesome performance, some of your support team may decide to take up the sport and try the Ironman themselves. It wouldn't be the first time that's happened. I was at one Ironman where three generations of one family finished the race. How amazing is that? A daughter, a father and a grandfather. Truly remarkable.

Ultimately being a bit selfish in a case like this is not such a bad thing, because in the end, everyone wins when you succeed and realize your Ironman dream.

(6) STILL NOT SURE? TRY VOLUNTEERING

Volunteering is a wise option if you are not quite ready to commit to your first Ironman Triathlon.

You may be unsure if the Ironman is a challenge you feel you want to undertake at this point in your life. There's no shame in that. It makes more sense to be certain before jumping into something like the Ironman that is so all consuming of time, energy, and monetary costs.

Pick a venue where you would like to make your first Ironman attempt when the time is right for you. Contact them and offer your services as a volunteer. I'm sure you will be welcomed with open arms.

If possible, take a week's holiday and volunteer for the days leading up to the race, as well as race day itself. This will give you an excellent feel for what the Ironman Triathlon is all about.

I'd highly recommend being out on the marathon or bike course as an aid station volunteer. Often there are aid stations that do double duty. You will see the athletes during the bike and the run. Believe me, if you needed a nudge to help make your commitment to enter the Ironman yourself, this will do it.

Perhaps the best place to be is right at the finish line. It may be difficult to get a spot here, but if you can, do it! Being in the transition area at the race finish is quite an experience. You'll be tripping over your feet as you run to sign up for the next year. It's a very moving experience.

There are several bonuses that go along with being a volunteer.

1) You witness first-hand ordinary people doing extraordinary things.

2) You are a HUGE part of them reaching their goal.

3) You get a really nifty volunteer t-shirt.

4) You will meet volunteers and athletes from all over the world.

5) You will most likely be able to go to the carbo dinner and awards for free.

6) Best of all, you can get up the morning after the race and enter for the next year and be assured of getting in. So make sure you bring your checkbook and necessary documentation.

You really can't lose by being a volunteer. Either you will be instrumental in helping others achieve their goals or possibly the volunteer experience will be the catalyst for you filling out an entry for the following year.

So don't feel pressured to do the Ironman right now! It will be there for you the next year or the year after that. It will call to you and when the time is right you will be truly "Ironstruck" and you will live the dream.

(7) SOME HAZARDS TO AVOID

It seems that every year there are more and more novice ironmen taking up the challenge of this great event.

I believe the biggest draw of the event is that it's within reach of anyone who is willing to put in the required effort to reach the finish line.

As a result it draws people from all walks of life as well a broad range of athletic ability.

I certainly would never want to deter anyone from striving for their Ironman goal, but it seems that little is ever written about the ever present hazards in an endurance event of this degree of difficulty. Make no mistake, it will test you to the limit of your physical, mental and emotional capabilities. It's finding out what we are truly made of that makes success such a triumph of the human spirit.

Unfortunate incidents do occur and it's important that everyone who plans to take up the this challenge be aware of and prepared for any contingency that might arise in training for, and racing in, their first Ironman.

The very first step, especially if you are not in great condition to start with, is to talk with your doctor and let him know what you have in mind. I would do this before you even start a training program. It can be extremely hazardous to stress yourself physically too much too soon.

Once you are into your training be sure to learn all you can about the equipment you will be using. This includes your bike, helmet, swim goggles, wetsuit, clothing and anything else that comes into play during Ironman training and racing.

Learn to ride in near proximity to others. Prepare mentally and physically to swim in the open water with upwards of 2000 other people. Also, it cannot be overstated how improper nutrition and hydration can be a recipe for disaster.

Here are just a few things I've witnessed over my 25 years as an endurance athlete.

In one marathon, a runner in front of me collapsed at about the 22 mile mark. I had noticed that he had slowed considerably over the previous mile. It was an extremely hot day. It turns out he had heat stroke and was rushed to the hospital and they had to get his core temperature down. He made several mistakes that day, as it turns out.

He wore no hat. He didn't drink enough. He went out way too fast for the conditions that day, and he wasn't properly trained for the distance.

At one Ironman Canada bike check-in (back when bike checks were mandatory) the bike mechanic checking a first-time Ironman's bike told him he had no rear brakes. (I mean, there were NO rear brakes.) The answer he got was, "well, I still have the front ones."

He is about to attempt an Ironman course with probably some of the fastest down hills of any race. I can just imagine him having to stop in a hurry at 80 kph with only front brakes.

I once watched two bikes wipe out on the course because a cyclist's water bottle was too loose in the cage and came flying out right under someone's wheel.

I was in one race where an athlete was given 5 units of intravenous in the medical tent because of dehydration. I'm still not sure if that's the record. Maybe it's six. Remember, if ambulance attendants give you an I.V. out on the course, your race is over. Be sure to drink enough. Don't let this happen to you.

The Ironman can be such a great experience. Don't let foolish mistakes mar your special day.

Here are some things to remember:

Have a thorough medical check-up before you even begin training. This is especially important if your fitness level is poor to start with. Many novice ironmen are runners or swimmers etc. and are already fit and will not be quite as much at risk.

If you are new to cycling, be sure and have a professional size the bike to fit you. Learn all you can about the mechanics and proper maintenance of your bike. Be sure to learn proper bike handling skills from an experienced cyclist. Be sure your helmet fits snugly and don't ever train without one.

On hot days, get used to wearing a cap of some sort and be sure to take in more fluids. A cap is great during those hot races. You can put water or ice in them at the aid stations.

If you begin to feel dizzy at all during a training run in the heat, slow down or stop and find some shade and take in fluids.

Many athletes have problems during the marathon because they don't take proper precautions during extreme heat. Even pros will slow down. They know better than to over exert themselves in adverse conditions.

Take advantage of the transition areas. Spending a few extra minutes to gather yourself between the bike and the run can pay dividends later in the day. It's not always the best idea to run straight from the bike to the marathon course.

The swim can be a harrowing experience for the novice Ironman. It need not be. Go in with a plan. Seed yourself properly or better yet, swim on the edges of the main pack and stay out of traffic trouble. Be sure you have trained sufficiently to easily manage the distance.

The Ironman might just be the most amazing thing you will ever experience. There are just so many positives that come out of this event.

Just some good old common sense and proper preparation will help you make the most of your day and ensure a safe, exciting race.

(8) 10 MOST COMMON 1ST IRONMAN MISTAKES

There's lots of trial and error involved when you're attempting your first Ironman. These days there's lots of advice floating around out there and it can get confusing at times. After over 20 years on the scene, I've seen some of the same mistakes made over and over again by first timers. Some of the same mistakes I made myself in the early years.

Here are the top ten mistakes that I feel you should really try and avoid. Just possibly it will give you a better shot at achieving your Ironman goal.

(1) OVERTRAINING

Almost without fail, the first time Ironman will go into the race overtrained. The hardest thing to learn about your training, is when to rest. It's really difficult to convince some athletes that rest is an essential component of their preparation. Some will insist on training no matter how tired they are or how sore they are. They will completely forget to factor in the physical and mental effort they expend at work every day. Worse yet, as the big day approaches, they will start their taper far too late. They continue to pound out the mileage for fear they'll lose the conditioning they worked so hard to achieve.

Here are a few tips: If you begin a workout, and just know it's going to be a struggle and you just have no energy, stop the workout and go home.

You obviously need more rest. When it gets really bad, take an entire weekend and do *nothing* associated with Ironman training. Go away for a few days. You won't lose a thing and will resume your training recovered and refreshed. As far as tapering, your longest workout day should be *4 weeks* before race day. Begin your taper there.

(2) POOR DIET

It's almost sad to see the effort some people put into their Ironman training only to stall their strength and endurance growth with an improper diet.

Avoid the junk food, eat a proper balance of complex carbs, protein and fat. Enhance a proper diet with vitamin supplements.

(3) IMPROPER FINAL WEEK PREPARATION

It's so easy to get caught up in the hype on Ironman week. Too much time is spent in restaurants eating food you don't normally eat. Far too many athletes will do the swim course several times or hammer out long bike rides or pound through ten mile runs in the blazing heat. None of this helps you. You must stay relaxed and get lots of rest that final week. Before you arrive at the venue, make sure you have a plan set out for the entire week, right up to race morning.

(4) IMPROPER PRE-RACE HYDRATION

Either athletes will drink too much or not enough leading up to the race. You should start hydrating several days before the race. The rule of thumb is, when urine is clear and copious, you are properly hydrated. Too much drinking will flush too many nutrients out of your system and could lead to hyponatremia. More is not better. *Don't* drink too much on race morning. You don't want fluid sloshing around in your stomach during the swim.

(5) IMPROPER RACE-EVE PREPARATION

The day before the race is crucial! You shouldn't be doing much of anything. Rest is the order of the day. Stay out of the sun. Eat your final large meal early in the day.(I never ate after 4 P.M. on that last day). This gives your digestive system time to work. Do what you must do. For instance, bike check-in and pre-race meeting. Take care of that and then go back to your room and relax.

(6) POOR SWIM STRATEGY

It's an Ironman tradition to have mass swim starts and I can't see that changing anytime in the near future. Most races have upwards of 2000 starters in a congested swim area. To convince yourself that the best strategy is to follow the course markers is a recipe for disaster. To decide to wait a minute or so, and then follow the markers is still a disaster. When you look around, there will be hundreds of others waiting as well. Go in with a workable strategy. Avoid the crush.

(7) MISTAKES IN TRANSITION

The last place you should be running is in the transition area. If this is your first race, there is absolutely nothing to be gained by it. It will drive your heart rate up. It will cause you to make mistakes. Take your time. In the chaos that surrounds you, keep in your own relaxed space.

(8) GOING OUT WAAAAY TOO FAST ON THE BIKE

Relax!! Don't eat or drink for twenty minutes or so. Let your body adjust to the new demands you're placing on it. Then begin to fuel up for the bike ahead and keep nutrition and fluid on an even keel for the entire bike ride. Spin at a nice relaxed pace for the first 40 km or so and then pick it up a little to the pace you feel you can maintain for the bulk of the ride.

(9) ABSOLUTELY NO RUN PLAN

Don't just go out and wing it. Have a well conceived run plan. Train months ahead for how you plan to handle the marathon. It's likely that not even 1% of first time Ironman hopefuls will run the entire marathon. So train for this. Do long run-walks in training. In other words, try a three hour training run like this.

Run for the first 30-45 minutes and then begin walking for two minutes and running for 12-15 minutes at a steady workable pace. Keep repeating this for the entire run. In effect, what you're doing, is practicing walking the aid stations and running in between as much as possible. When you begin the bike to run transition try and get in as much mileage as you can before you begin walking.

(10) ABSOLUTELY NO EATING OR DRINKING PLAN FOR THE RUN

As the marathon progress and your energy and endurance are being challenged to the max, the normal reaction is to try eating a bit of everything available at the aid stations. This is another disaster in the making. The last thing you need is cookies, fruit, and coke, etc. trashing your stomach. If you trained all year with gels and a certain type of replacement drink, then that's what you should stick with. Don't make the mistake of searching everywhere for a miracle cure. It isn't there. The Ironman hurts. That is the nature of the beast. Don't let it get the best of you. Fight through it with an eating and drinking plan that you've thought out long before race day.

I would be particularly concerned with having a proper diet and overall race plan. Take the guesswork out of race day. Know exactly what your swim plan will be. Proper diet and vitamin supplements are a must. Make sure your Ironman plans cover everything up to and including the race.

(9) DIET FOR AN IRONMAN

Training diets come in dozens of shapes and sizes. It will just make you crazy! Trying to figure out what to eat and what not to eat. Especially when you start doing some serious training and you are HUNGRY when you get home. Well the good news is that I've tried pretty well all of the major diets over the years (and some not so major) and can cut out much of the guesswork for you. And no, I don't have a degree in nutrition. I earned my credentials in the kitchen and at the dinner table.

In the early years most of us Ironman beginners had no clue about diets. Most of us used the world famous, much loved seafood diet. You see food and you eat it.

However, after a few years it started to dawn on me how important diet was when training for an event as physically demanding as the Ironman. I think I can honestly say that I took something good out of every diet I ever tried. Well almost.

A few years ago, I tried one diet for 4 months that maintained all you needed was lots of protein and not much carbo. Against my better judgement but just to see what would happen, I gave it at try.

After 4 months on this diet, I entered a 10km race and shortly after the gun went off (oh, about 5-6 seconds) I knew I was in trouble. I had zero energy and of the over the dozens of 10km races I have entered over the years this was my worst time by far.

I think I can say with certainty that an endurance athlete should never go on a high protein, high fat, low carb diet! It may work for a segment of the population, but is certainly not meant for everyone.

From all the reading I've done, and all the diets I've tried, I'm 100% certain that carbohydrates are the key to the ideal Ironman Triathlon diet. I'm not talking simple carbs here. Really try and avoid sugar. Stay away from those cakes, cookies, ice cream and chocolate. For the year or so you dedicate to accomplishing your Ironman dream, stay focused on your diet. Trust me, it will be all that much more fun to indulge when it's all over.

If anything, I went overboard on the carbohydrate scale. It was a major part of my diet. It isn't for everyone. Just make sure that on a percentage basis that your carbohydrates are always higher then your protein and fat intake. Try and keep your protein and fat at about the same percentages. Some of the best carbohydrate sources are pasta, brown rice, whole wheat bread, pretty well all vegetables and a controlled amount of fruit because they have lots of sugar. I found I was making one major mistake though. I always used white pasta and ate tons of potatoes because I knew they were one of the purest forms of carbohydrate. Much to my surprise a few years ago my doctor said my bad cholesterol was too high. After talking about my diet we narrowed it down to too many high sugar carbohydrates. The white pasta I ate every day and all the potatoes. So now I ALWAYS use whole wheat pasta and I cut out potatoes and substitute with sweet potatoes. Problem solved.

For protein you have several preferable choices. Egg whites are awesome. Give the yolks to your neighbor who is on that OTHER diet. Or have scrambled eggs with 3 egg whites and one entire egg. Limit yourself to 3 or 4 whole eggs per week. From the Dairy aisle your best bets are low fat cottage cheese, plain yogurt (not those fruity ones) and skim milk. From the meat aisle (if you eat meat) chicken and turkey white meat (yes, and take that skin off-that's where most of the fat is stored), and a small amount of lean beef maybe once, but not more than twice a week. Fish of course is just a great choice. There is nothing wrong with canned tuna or salmon. Don't forget about legumes, and also soya products are a staple now of many triathletes.

The fat part of your diet will often be found in the protein you eat. There will be fat in the cottage cheese and the chicken or turkey or beef you might eat. There will be fat in the 3 or 4 whole eggs you eat every week if you choose to. There will be a small amount of fat in the skim milk. Fish will also provide some fat, and I know it's expensive, but salmon is awesome for protein and fat (Omega oil). The oil I preferred and used for years is virgin olive oil. That is, until I came across coconut oil. Now I use both. A less expensive option is canola oil. Try having vinegar, olive oil and coconut oil tossed in your salad and top it with cottage cheese. A great example of complex carbs, good fat and protein.

Some notes: condiments (ketchup, mustard, mayonnaise, salad dressings etc) should be used sparingly. Cheddar cheese is fine, but try and stick to 6-8 ounces per week. Your best cheeses are hard cheeses. Number one choice is parmesan (grated) for your pasta. I would avoid jam because of the sugar content. Peanut butter is o.k. in controlled amounts if you buy the real thing that has a half inch of oil on the top and is a pain to mix (but hey! that means it's the right one). Avoid using the peanut butter that has icing sugar mixed in it and no oil on the top. Icing sugar is sometimes added to make it smooth for you to save you mixing it at home.

As far as your beverage choices, use skim milk as I mentioned above. Don't be afraid of aspartame. It is a far better choice than sugar and allows you to use sweeteners in your coffee etc. So that means you can drink diet pop on occasion (with aspartame) Another really good choice is Crystal Lite (they also use aspartame) if you prefer a sweeter option to water. Also, whoever said drink 6 or 8 glasses of water a day, has got to be kidding. I would have to GAG down that much water every day. Good news though. I read recently that after extensive studies, (by someone) drinks like coffee, tea and soft drinks are now included in the 6-8 glasses of water.

I've discovered that what you eat really goes a long way to determining how thirsty you are and how much water you drink. I believe if you eat an extraordinary amount of carbohydrates like I do, you require less water. Don't forget, fresh vegetables for instance are up around 75-80% water.

And I have a huge salad every day. Beer or wine is o.k. in extreme moderation. Maybe three drinks a week and drink light beer. Getting drunk is not a great idea when you are training. It causes dehydration and could well ruin your next few days of workouts.

A few important notes: Don't get me wrong. When you are out on long rides and runs of 2 hours duration and more, be very sure you have lots of water or some type of fluid replacement. Don't go overboard on drinking water while training however. More and more information is coming out about athletes taking too much water and flushing out too many nutrients and causing physical problems as a result.

Also: As far as the amount you eat.

You are training for an Ironman and will burn tons of calories. When I mention diet, I'm not talking the amounts you eat. I'm talking about the food you choose to eat. Trust me. One day if you go for a training swim followed closely by a 50 or 60 mile bike ride, you are going to be hungry. Don't worry yourself about how much you eat. When you are really training, your body will tell you how much you need to eat. I like to call it my "appestat."

I have *never* measured, or worried about the amount I eat when I'm in training. I am 150-155 pounds and eat tons!! I know everyone has a different metabolism, but just the same, you will know darn well when you have had a hard training day. Eat accordingly.

In many sports, not just triathlon, athletes will train religiously for months and not realize their full potential because of an improper diet.

Don't let this happen to you.

(10) HAVE YOU TRIED COCONUT OIL?

Over the years I've always been on the lookout for a diet or diet supplement that would enhance my training and improve my race times.

It was almost by chance that I happened upon coconut oil and its use as a diet supplement. I was cruising the net one day and came across an article on the subject and like many other intriguing diet "ideas" I've stumbled upon in the past, decided to give it a try.

I've always believed that I had no business writing about any diet unless I had tried it myself. To my way of thinking that's the only way to pass on relevant, honest information to readers. As a result I've tried a variety of different diets and supplements over the years and coconut oil is one of them.

To be quite honest, I was just blown away by the results I experienced when I incorporated coconut oil into my training diet.

First a bit of science behind the coconut diet:

Coconut oil is comprised of fatty acids called "medium chain triglycerides" or MCT'S. In nature, coconut oil has the largest concentration of these MCT'S outside of human breast milk. Vegetable oils, on the other hand, are made up primarily of "long chain fatty acids" or LCT'S.

For quite some time now scientific literature has claimed that LCT'S tend to produce fat in the body, while MCT'S promote what is called "thermogenesis". Thermogenesis increases the body's metabolism, producing energy.

This has been common knowledge in the animal feed business for years. It you feed animals vegetable oil, they gain weight and produce more fatty meat. If you feed them coconut oil, they will be very lean.

Tests on rats published in "The American Journal of Clinical Nutrition" concluded that MCT rats gained 15% less weight than rats fed LCT'S. The conclusion:

MCT diets result in decreased body fat related to increased metabolic rate and thermogenesis.

Similar tests were conducted on humans at Vanderbilt University in 1989 with the same basic results.

Regardless of scientific study result, I prefer to try these things on my own and see the results firsthand.

Over twenty years of competition and numerous diets, the LEAST I ever weighed was 150-151 pounds. This was my competition weight. If I were to weigh myself on any given race morning, my weight would be in this range, give or take a pound. That all changed when I included coconut oil in my diet.

I weighed myself on the first day of the diet as I always did when I tried something new, and wouldn't step on a scale again for one month. I live by that rule when trying a new diet. My start weight was as usual, 151 lbs.

I added 5 tablespoons of coconut oil per day to my meals. Usually when you buy coconut oil it will be solidified. I just leave mine at room temperature and in few days the whole container is liquefied. I don't store it in the fridge because it will solidify again. If it is solid, it's easy enough to melt down into liquid form.

I added it to my oatmeal in the morning, to my pasta, and used it in smoothies. I always use olive oil in my salads and started adding 2 tablespoons of coconut oil to every salad. It's an amazingly versatile product. You can easily come up with your own cooking uses for it.

When you use it in food it's not an unpleasant taste and most of the time you won't even know it's there. Combine it with your food anyway you like, but aim for at least 5 tablespoons a day and stick with it. Like any diet, there's really not much point even starting unless you're committed to it.

Well, I did this for exactly one month. Then I stepped back on the scale. WOW! 142 pounds!

I was 10 pounds lower than I had been over the past 20 years! I *could not* believe it. Remember that for the month I used coconut oil, I was in full training. Any diet you ever try should be done in conjunction with a fitness regimen. So I believe this is an ideal addition to any Ironman's diet. Or ANY athlete's diet for that matter.

A few things I noticed:

Along with losing weight, my energy level increased.

Even though I lost 10 pounds, I seemed to have the same amount of overall strength. This is crucial to an athlete. What makes some athletes so amazing is their strength to weight ratio. In other words, you can be a 120 pound woman, but be very strong for that weight. Take it a step further and imagine the consequences if you become 110 lbs and don't lose any strength and have increased energy.

Imagine yourself running a marathon carrying a 10 pound bag of potatoes on your back. Now imagine running the same marathon without the bag of potatoes and more energy.

A perfect example of what I mean by strength to weight ratio is Lance Armstrong.

When he was fighting cancer he lost tons of weight of course, but when he won that battle and became healthy, he never did gain back all of the weight that he originally had. Yet, he became stronger. In other words, his strength to weight ratio changed big time. It seems that his body chemistry changed for the better.

When I watched him climb those endless mountain passes in the Tour, I'm just amazed at how lean and strong he is. Also, how high his energy level is.

Of course we can't all be the exceptional athlete Lance is, but I truly believe that incorporating coconut oil into ones diet can have a profound effect on any athletes training and racing results.

(11) PROPER HYDRATION

For years athletes were told to drink as much as they possibly could before a long endurance event such as the marathon.

Dehydration had to be avoided at all costs.

This line of reasoning has been seriously altered over the past several years.

The dangers of hyponatremia or "drinking more than you are using" are now front and center. Hyponatremia in a worst case scenario can lead to coma and even death.

Hyponatremia is caused by drinking so much that you dilute the sodium content of your blood.

Some of the signs are nausea, headache, muscle cramps, confusion and seizures. Medical help as soon as possible is imperative.

According to a Mayo Clinic fitness specialist, endurance athletes used to drink enough to "stay ahead" of their thirst. As a result, they were drinking more than they were losing through sweating.

Of course you can't allow yourself to become dehydrated, as that brings on a whole new set of complications. The key is to take in as much fluid as you use and keep an even balance.

The International Marathon Medical Directors Association recommends that, during extended exercise, athletes drink no more than 31 ounces of water per hour.

That seems to fall exactly in line with one of the best Ironman results I ever experienced.

I used one full water bottle between aid stations on the bike. During the run all I took from the aid stations was one cup of water. I took nothing else to eat or drink for the marathon. Assuming the cups hold around 5 ounces of water and the aid stations were 1 mile apart and I was running an 8:30 pace, my intake was pretty well right on 30 ounces per hour.

It doesn't seem like much fluid, but it was perfectly balanced I guess because the marathon time was 3:34 and I never had any sort of hydration problem during the entire run. So I suppose I luckily hit right on the perfect balance and what I took in was what I was using.

So, some things to remember:

Don't "over-hydrate" before the race start. I don't believe you should feel fluid sloshing around in your stomach. Also, you shouldn't have a bloated feeling. If that's the case, you've probably taken on more fluid than necessary. Plus for the Ironman, it makes for an uncomfortable swim.

Drink enough to avoid dehydration. Don't under compensate. It's a fine line between dehydration and hyponatremia. Experimenting with your fluid intake will help you find what's best for you.

According to studies, the correct optimum amount of fluid intake is approximately 31 ounces per hour of sustained physical activity.

The chances of dehydration are greater than hyponatremia, but both can lead to serious complications, so finding the proper fluid intake balance for you cannot be overstated.

(12) TAKE YOUR VITAMINS

There are a host of choices for supplementing your Ironman diet. I'll mention a few that I found helpful to my training and racing. I won't delve too deeply into the world of vitamins. This is an area best left to the experts. As I said earlier, if I have not used a product or diet or anything else concerning Ironman training, I won't recommend it. Here are a few of the supplements I had good success with.

I always made a point of including the anti-oxidants vitamin C, Vitamin E and Selenium to my list of vitamins. Actually I would buy the vitamin C with Selenium added. Their main function was to act as a deterrent to the forming of free radicals in your body when you eat unsaturated fats.

It seemed that every few years, Ironman Canada featured a *really* cold swim. It doesn't bother a lot of people, but I had quite a hard time with it. Being super low in body fat has its disadvantages. I came across the vitamin supplement pantothenic acid that plays an important role in energy production. I also discovered that pantothenic acid is a key antioxidant for athletes who compete in extreme conditions, especially cold water. I added it to my vitamin choices and never had problems with cold water again. If the location of your first Ironman is in a part of the world where warm water is no guarantee, I would highly recommend using it. Otherwise it probably isn't a necessary choice for you. If you do purchase it, what you ask for is calcium pentathonate, the calcium salt of pantothenic acid.

I also noticed an improvement in energy levels when I used branch chain amino acids. Amino acids, the molecules that make up every protein in our foods and bodies and can also function as anti-oxidants. I believe this vitamin supplement would be valuable to almost anyone doing the intense training demanded to prepare properly for an Ironman. It also compensates if your diet is a bit lacking in protein. I was on such a high carb diet, that this choice was ideal for me.

My all-time favorite for a supplement is L'carnatine. I would use this one and three weeks later be five pounds lighter. I also notice a marked improvement in my energy level and recovery from training. If it's within your means and if you can find the product, I would give it a try. It is *very* expensive, but well worth it. I believe it's available over the counter in the U.S., but is actually available only by prescription in Canada.

So there you have it. That is the same vitamin package I use leading up to an Ironman. It took years of hit and miss to finally come up with this combination. All the doses except for Vitamin C and Selenium were 500 mgs. I would take more (1000) vitamin C with 50 mgs of Selenium added.

Regardless, anyone doing the demanding training needed to improve their Ironman chances should seriously consider vitamin supplements.

NOTE: Don't fall into this trap. If something works really well for you, don't assume that more will be even better. Stay with the amount that seemed to make a difference.

(13) WEIGHT TRAINING

For many people "doing" weights is a scary thought. They really feel they will be terribly out of place with all those muscle bound types in the weight room.

I agree that was the case years ago, but not anymore. You'll even find seniors pushing the weights since it was discovered how weight training can better their quality of life.

I don't claim to be a fitness expert, but I will tell you what exercises and what format worked for me after many years of trial and error doing weights.

Some tips about doing weights...

I narrowed it down to six exercises. Three for upper body and three for lower body.

UPPER BODY- Lat pull-downs, arm curls and bench press...These exercises will add some strength and flexibility for your swimming.

LOWER BODY- Squats, Quad extensions and Hamstring curls...These exercises will improve your running especially on hills and they will also help pretty well every aspect of your biking.

Do weights three times per week (not more) and always have a rest day in between.

Do three sets of each exercise and do ten reps each time.

Always use machines as opposed to free-weights. It's much safer, especially if you're new to the weight room.

Always use your first set for warm-up and use very light weight. Do all three sets of one exercise before moving on to the next one.

For your second sets add a small amount of weight (2-5 lbs.). After the second ten reps you should feel a bit of a burn. If you can complete the third set fairly easily, increase the weight of your second and third sets next weight training day. Always leave your warm-up set at a very light weight. When you get to the point that you can't finish the third set, then stay at that weight until you do. That's how you will tell if you are getting stronger.

NOTE -- You should record the amount of weight you are at so you don't forget the next time out.

There's really no need to spend more than 35-45 minutes in the weight room. You want to get in there, do your six exercises and get out. You only need about 90 seconds rest between reps. You have too many other things to do. Get in the pool instead and work on your nice long smooth stroke. Besides, swimming after a weight work-out feels great. I always planned a swim for after weights.

I've always felt that the best exercise in the entire gym for Ironman over-all improvement is the squat. Be CERTAIN to do this exercise. If all the time you have on any given day is 10-15 minutes, then do just squats. Be careful to do them properly. Use a squat station, not free weights! Make sure you get the technique right. Straight back, feet shoulder width apart, toes pointed slightly out. If you've never done a squat before in your life have one of the fitness people in the gym show you proper technique. You could easily hurt your back by using improper technique. Don't be afraid to wear a squat belt. It will help you maintain your form and keep a straight back as you lower into the squat position. This is critical. Proper squat technique will do wonders for your cycling.

*** I once read an interview of the Puntos twins who were both excellent swimmers and runners. They said their cycling never really improved a lot until they went to the gym and did squats. In 1984 they were first and second woman in the Hawaii Ironman.

IMPORTANT: You can REALLY injure yourself if you try and do too much weight too soon. Don't feel self-conscious because everyone around you is pushing big weights. They have different goals than you. Look at the big picture and what you are trying to accomplish in the end. How many of them will be able to add Ironman to their name? Focus on the task at hand.

(14) WEIGHT ROOM ETIQUETTE

If it's your first time adding weight training to your fitness program, you may not be quite sure of proper weight room etiquette.

Hopefully I can offer a few suggestions that may aid you in avoiding a few of the more common pitfalls.

-- First of all, make sure you're dressed properly. Most facilities insist on proper attire and as a rule it's pretty standard. Basically, they don't want you walking in there in street clothes. Also, they expect the guys to keep their tops on. The most important consideration is proper footwear. Improper footwear can lead to slipping and sliding and possible injury.

-- The towels and spray you see beside most weight stations is there for good reason. It's proper etiquette to wipe down a station after you use it. It's pretty uncomfortable and a bit gross to use equipment covered with another person's sweat. It can also be a health hazard.

-- If someone's doing a workout in front of a mirror, don't walk between that person and the mirror. People do it all the time and it's extremely rude.

-- Don't put a water bottle, towel or piece of clothing, or anything else for that matter on a weight bench or piece of equipment you're not using. Basically you're preventing anyone else from using that equipment. Set these items down on the floor next to the equipment you are using.

-- Don't start a conversation with, or interrupt in any other way, someone who is in the middle of lifting a weight. I see people do this and just can't understand it. You can easily cause them to lose concentration and injure themselves.

-- Be sure to replace any weights or other equipment to where it belongs after use. This is possibly the pet peeve of any weight room, anywhere.

-- Don't interrupt someone to let them know that they're doing an exercise all wrong. All that does is embarrass people. If they want to know, it's best to let them ask for help on their own.

-- Dropping weights to the floor with a great deal of crashing and banging is a distraction to everyone around you and can also cause damage to the equipment or the floor. If you can't have it in control when you're setting it down, then obviously it's too heavy for you. Use less weight.

-- Also high on the pet peeve scale in any weight room is the loud grunting and groaning that's meant to impress others and show them how strong you are. Actually, I think it does the exact opposite.

-- Some people insist on using the same piece of equipment for half an hour without considering that others may be waiting to use it. I would suggest that you should try and use fifteen minutes as a maximum guideline for any one station. Actually, some weight rooms have signs posted to that effect.

-- Finally, if you're not sure how to use a certain piece of equipment, it's always best to ask one of the weight room attendants who are there for that reason. Often other people are on a schedule and it's best not to distract them from their workout. Also, they may not be qualified to give you advice on proper technique. The same applies if you want someone to spot for you.

I hope that if you are a first time weight room user that some of these pointers might be helpful to you.

Good luck with your weight training program.

(15) MASSAGE THERAPY

Massage therapy is something else to consider when preparing for you first Ironman Triathlon. For some reason, there are those who benefit more than others from massage. I have tried it, but found it a bit expensive to be able to include it as a weekly part of my training. I used it more as a reward after 6 or 8 weeks of hard training.

Should you decide to include massage therapy as a regular component of your training, be sure to find someone skilled in "sports massage" which in many cases is a deeper massage than most people are used to.

There's no doubt that a massage can do wonders after a long bike or run session, but I wouldn't recommend it too soon *before* a planned long training day. I always found that I was so relaxed, I didn't want to do anything after a massage.

It's for this reason I would *never* get a massage too soon before a major race day like the Ironman. If you want a pre-race massage I would highly recommend getting it several days before the big race.

If you only have one massage all year, there is one you must make a point of not missing out on. It's the free one you get right after they put that finishers medal around your neck. Just tell that volunteer who is "supporting" you that you would like to go to the massage tent. They will make sure you get there. Get there as soon as can after crossing the line as it tends to get pretty busy depending on your arrival time. You may have to sign in and take a seat, but normally you won't be left waiting too long.

Different things work for different people and possibly your best option is to give sports massage a try and see if it enhances your recovery and training. At the very least, treat yourself to a massage as a reward for all your dedicated training.

(16) WHAT ABOUT A CHIROPRACTOR?

For years chiropractors were seldom given the credit they deserved when it came to improving athletic performance. Now however, it's not uncommon at all to see chiropractors treating world class athletes. Several years ago I decided to try chiropractic adjustments because I was developing problem areas from my Ironman Triathlon training. The most bothersome was a constantly sore neck from all the swimming I was doing. Also, I had upper back and shoulder pain from cycling in the profile position.

After making inquiries, I soon had the name of a chiropractic doctor who specialized in treating a wide range of athletes. I remember sitting in his waiting room on the day of my first appointment and seeing autographed pictures on his wall. Pro hockey players, bobsled teams and professional dancers had all been treated by him. It looked like I was in the right place.

After just one treatment I had relief from my neck pain and my next swim was a lot more enjoyable. From what the doctor told me, my spine was out of alignment and he recommended a course of treatment that would keep everything well-adjusted during the Ironman training season.

Note: Most chiropractors will suggest you come in 4 or 5 times a week. Mine did as well, but only for the first 2 weeks so he could get the adjustments to "hold." It's not really feasible or necessary to have that many appointments week after week. After 2 weeks we set up a schedule of twice a week. It was perfect. You seldom have to wait and the adjustments themselves only take 10 or 15 minutes. I found the treatments quite affordable as well. Where I live the provincial health plan pays part of the cost and the patient pays the rest (about $20 per visit). It was one of the best training decisions I ever made and the $160 a month was money well spent.

From that point on, I was a patient until the doctor retired. He used to say he was giving me a competitive edge and I believed him. I had my best Ironman Triathlon result ever the first year chiropractic adjustments became part of my training program. It was one of the highlights of my Ironman career when the doctor asked me to autograph a finish line picture for him. From then on it was on the wall between the Olympic bobsled team and the pro hockey player.

I highly recommend you include chiropractic adjustments as part of your training program for your first Ironman Triathlon. At the very least, try a few adjustments and see what they do for you.

(17) HEART RATE MONITOR TRAINING

A heart rate monitor can be an excellent training tool. In a nutshell, following a heart rate monitor program teaches your body to burn fat as opposed to carbs. It teaches to be aerobic as opposed to anaerobic.

AEROBIC - Workouts where you are burning fat as your source of energy.

ANAEROBIC - Workouts where you burn carbs as your source of energy.

For an event like the Ironman, where endurance is paramount, teaching your body to burn fat is ideal for a very simple reason.

Your body stores a lot more fat than it does carbs. So during your race, if you burn fat and not carbs, you don't use up your glycogen stores too quickly. Glycogen, simply put, is stored carbs. Believe me. In a physically demanding event like the Ironman, once you use up your glycogen stores, you will hit the proverbial wall with the force of truck. Your pace will slow and even walking will become extremely uncomfortable.

A heart monitor will guide you in staying in your fat burning range. There is a reliable formula for finding your maximum aerobic heart rate. The idea is to NOT go over this heart rate in the early months of your training. If you are in poor shape to start with, you will be training at a very slow pace at first. If the program is done properly, you will find that eventually you will be able to train at a faster pace and still stay below your max. Also, by staying out of the anaerobic zone, your recoveries from training will be much faster and less painful. Better still, your chances of being injured will be diminished. I have trained with a heart rate monitor for years and have had great success. I would highly recommend giving it a try.

If you decide to, here is how to figure out your maximum aerobic heart rate:

The key number is 180. Subtract your age (no cheating).

When you begin, if your physical fitness really sucks (and don't worry, we'll change that) take off ten more beats.

If you have trained a few days a week for several years, don't change the number.

If you have trained like an all star for a few years and are in really good shape to start, add five beats.

If you are almost set to retire (over 60), add five beats.

If you are still in your teens, add five beats.

Now that you have that magic number, your maximum aerobic heart rate, strap on that monitor, and away you go. I would suggest using the monitor in the run and bike portions of your Ironman training. It doesn't work that well in the pool, because you basically have to stop to check your monitor. It's pretty difficult to track while you're swimming.

Use it on all your runs for sure and always start out running slowly for 10 or 15 minutes, then let your heart rate get to within 20-25 beats below your maximum. If you are in really poor shape, it will seem very slow to you. That's o.k.! Be patient. It will improve. Over the weeks you will teach your body to burn fat and like magic you will start running faster without going over your max. Here is how to do a test so you can actually see your progress. Do your initial test the first few days you start heart rate monitor training.

Find somewhere (a track etc.) where you can run an exact measured mile.

Warm up for 15 minutes and stay 20-25 beats below your max. After your warm-up, pick up speed so that when you hit the start line for your mile, you are right on your maximum aerobic heart rate.

Begin your stop watch when you hit the start line. Stay in a very tight range for the whole mile. For example, if your max. rate is 130, stay between 125 and 135 through the whole test. The idea is to average 130 beats per minute, your maximum rate. Stop your timer right at the end of the mile. Record that time.

In one month and not before, do the exact test again. If you have trained on a regular basis (4-5 times a week) and used the monitor properly you will see an improvement.

FOR EXAMPLE: If your first test resulted in a mile time of 9 min 40 seconds and your second test had a time of 9 min 15 seconds, then congratulations! You are teaching your body to burn fat. You are becoming fitter! You are training at the very same heart rate as when you started, but are able run faster without any added stress.

Do the test every month (not every week). Your mile time will continue to drop and your fitness level will improve as well if you train on a regular basis. After 4 months or so when you have developed a sound aerobic base, you will be able to start adding some anaerobic work-outs. This is an indication that you have come a long way.

(18) SHOULD YOU STRETCH?

Stretching is one of those grey areas that nobody seems to really understand. Sometimes I watch people stretching just before a race and you can just tell they are going through the motions--unsure exactly what it is they're doing.

I tried the stretching thing for a year or so and came to the conclusion that for me it was a waste of time. Actually more to the point, it did more harm than good. I injured myself twice while stretching and ended up missing training time.

There's really enough preparation work for an Ironman hopeful to do and I think you can forgo the stretching routine. I think stretching might be a good thing if it were done every day, but ultimately that just doesn't happen. I watch young kids in swim clubs who stretch every day for quite a long time and that makes sense. Their bodies are used to it and it is part of their everyday routine.

It makes more sense to me to swim, bike or run slowly at the beginning of a training session for at least 10-15 minutes and let your muscles stretch out naturally by doing exactly what they will be doing in a few minutes at a faster pace.

That is my advice to you. If you stretch now and have a regular program and it works for you, then you should stick with it. Otherwise I wouldn't even start.

(19) SO GUYS. ABOUT LEG SHAVING

For guys, shaving their legs for the big race has pretty well become an important part of Ironman race preparation. It's right up there with carbo loading and pre-race hydration.

Actually, more to the point, it's become a tradition and the mark of a real honest to God triathlete who has truly arrived. Well, at least in the minds of some.

I doubt if all novice ironmen actually realize why leg-shaving takes place and why the heck they're putting themselves through it in the first place.

At least in the beginning there was one and only one logical reason to shave your legs for an Ironman. It all started with cyclists who shave their legs all the time in the event they have one of those nasty crashes where exposed skin meets the asphalt highway. It's far easier to clean and treat road-rash if the blood and dirt isn't dried and matted into your hair. Actually, it works. I've crashed a few times and it's surprising just how much faster these abrasions actually heal when the affected area is smooth and easy to treat.

I came to realize early in my career that there's also another very good time to shave not just your legs, but your arms and chest and stomach as well. It was my very first Ironman in Hawaii in 1984 when I ran into this guy who had been a competitive swimmer for years. He talked about four of us into shaving all our body hair off. He actually arranged for a hair salon in Kona to shave us all after they closed for the day. (All it cost was three bottles of wine). Then he insisted that we go back to our rooms and use a razor and shave with it as well. This in effect was taking all the hair stubble off leaving a completely smooth surface. He insisted this be done the eve of the race, not before. This, he said, was something competitive swimmers did all the time.

Well, I couldn't believe it when the gun went off and I hit the water race morning. I had never experienced a feeling like it. I literally glided through the water. It was like all resistance was gone and it suddenly seemed effortless to propel myself forward. In that moment it became abundantly clear to me why fish don't have hair. You virtually *slide* through the water. After all that training, it was such a bonus to have this extra advantage on race morning.

I highly recommend it, but of course if you are wearing a wetsuit, all bets are off. It has to be a "no wetsuit" swim.

As stated earlier, the only real reason to shave your legs otherwise, is to make cleaning abrasions easier. Well, some also claim it's cooler visually and temperature wise, I guess.

There are those who honestly believe shaving their legs makes them bike faster, but that's a stretch. But hey, if it makes you feel faster, go for it. Actually, I've tried Ironman Canada with and without shaving and really, I don't believe bike times are any faster and and speed advantage is in one's head.

So, should you shave your legs before that first Ironman? Sure, why not. If it makes you feel more like an Ironman then of course you should. That's if you don't mind taking the time and putting up with that itching when the hair starts to grow back.

Should you shave completely (not your head, by the way) for a no wetsuit swim? Without a doubt, YES. It's an advantage.

(20) SWIM EQUIPMENT

Your Ironman swim equipment includes some items that are optional and some that are essential.

Optional for training are pull buoys, hand paddles, kick boards, and swim fins...

PULL BUOYS - Like most rookie swimmers with low body fat, my legs would sink way to low in the water. I assumed I needed the buoys to keep my feet up and my body in a more or less stream-lined position. They also gave me a false sense of security and put added stress on my arms and shoulders.

HAND PADDLES - Quite often these are used in combination with pull buoys. Using these two together gave me shoulder injury and I missed 2 weeks of training in the pool.

KICK BOARDS - I just dreaded these things. Maybe in about 5 minutes I could do one length in the pool, but sometimes I would actually go backwards. If someone ever tries to hand you one of these...RUN!! RUN AS FAST AS YOU CAN!!

SWIM FINS - These can be useful when used at the proper time. When I was really concentrating on a particular drill, which sometimes meant slow forward speed, I would use swim fins.

CONCLUSION: I have used all of these pieces of swim equipment, and would suggest you don't use any of them except for maybe swim fins when working on your stroke. Learn the proper balance and buoyancy without any swimming aids and you will be far better off. Plus kicking isn't really that big of an issue for your Ironman swim if your swim stroke is smooth and efficient.

**** NOTE: I have no wish to undermine any swim coach or the training plan he has devised. I am just passing on to you what I have discovered over years of doing all the wrong things in the pool. If you are in a swim program and your coach uses all the above mentioned tools, then stick with it if you are happy with the results.

SWIM SUITS - Don't make the mistake of spending big money on swimsuits. On average I went through about four pair in a training year. If you are pool training (and probably most of you are) chlorine makes no distinction between expensive and bargain priced swim suits. It eats them all equally.

SWIM GOGGLES - It would be wise to try several different types of swim goggles. When you find a pair that feel really comfortable, don't leak, and don't fog up---put them away for your Ironman. I would recommend the large style of swim goggle that gives you wider vision. Also I would get them tinted in case of direct sun or reflection that can be very irritating.

LENS ANTI-FOG - Just to be safe, I always used this. It can't hurt to be cautious. Put it on your swim glass lenses race morning to "guarantee" you won't have fogging problems.

WETSUITS - You can and should use these in every Ironman race, unless of course your first race is in Hawaii or some other tropical location. They do tend to give you more speed, because there is less friction, but the main function is to keep you warm and at the same time, make you look cool. They can be expensive, but I would consider giving the Internet a try. There are many very good companies that sell quality wetsuits and are knowledgeable about their product. However, Internet shopping means you can't try it on before purchase and this can be a problem. Proper fitting of a wetsuit is vital.

NOTE: As a rule, wetsuits do feel a bit tight and constricting out of the water, but are more comfortable in the water.

(21) BIKE EQUIPMENT

Without a doubt the bike equipment you choose can greatly influence the outcome of your first Ironman.

However, don't believe for a moment that the more expensive the bike, the easier and faster your bike split will be. The most important factor, and one that is often overlooked, is having the bike you choose sized just for you. Most bike outlets will supply this service. I just can't stress how important this is. A proper fit means you will be getting full use of the proper muscle groups and will have a smooth, circular pedal stroke. Most importantly, it can make for a much more comfortable transition into the run.

Also, when you consider it, there's not much point in spending thousands of dollars more for a bike because it is a pound or two lighter when you're going to be packing five pounds of water and food on it for the race. For your first race I would suggest a good reliable mid-priced bike. You can always upgrade if you choose to continue on with the sport in the following years.

Here's something to think about. In Kona 1984, on a brutally hot and windy day, there were two cyclists under the 5 hour mark. Dave Scott was 5:11 and went on to run a 2:53 marathon and ultimately won the race. My point is, pretty well any mid-range priced bike you buy will be 10 times better than what these guys raced on that day. Think about it. Aerobars would have been a huge advantage that day. Today, we have clipless pedals, but back then there was no such thing. Everyone had the old toe clips. The bikes were much heavier. The tires were nowhere near as good as we can get now. There is just no comparison.

Ultimately your training, preparation, athletic ability, and courage are equally important ingredients to a successful Ironman bike.

There are other pieces of bike equipment that are also very important.

PROFILE BARS - I don't believe they have invented an Ironman race yet that has no wind. Profile bars are a *must* to reduce wind resistance and conserve your energy for the upcoming marathon. If possible, try and have your shift levers mounted at the very front of your profile bars where your hands meet. That way you're not sitting up or reaching down to shift gears. I have something called "swift shifters." They are just perfect for the Ironman bike.

CYCLE COMPUTER - Some bike computers have way too many functions. All you need is cadence, speed, and an odometer to tell how far you've gone. That way you're not forever pushing buttons to find the proper setting.

CLIPLESS PEDALS AND SHOES TO FIT - These were just a great invention. They are so easy to get in and out of and allow for a much smoother and more economical pedal stroke than the old clips we started out with. It's very important to have the tension set just right. You want to be able to get into them easily, yet not have your foot snap out at the worst possible time. (Like climbing a hill for instance.) If you ski, it's sort of the same idea as ski bindings. Just keep experimenting with it until you have to give your ankle a fairly quick, sharp twist for your shoe to come away from the pedal. That way you know it's not set too loose. Also, make sure the bike has forward momentum when twisting out of the pedal. If you are almost stopped you could fall right over.

BOTTLE CAGES - Personally, I carry 4 water bottles. One inside the handlebars with a flexible plastic straw so I can drink without removing the bottle, one in the standard position on the frame, and a two bottle cage behind the seat. The water bottle on the frame and the two behind the seat were for my electrolyte replacement drink. The bottle with the plastic straw was water. It had a top that snapped open, but stayed attached and at aid stations I would just refill it with water if needed. When I wanted a replacement drink, I would take it from the bottle on the bike frame. When it was empty I would switch it with a full bottle from behind the seat. If I thought I would need more than three bottles, I would leave one or two at the special needs station.

If what you normally use for a replacement drink is being supplied on the race course, then you can do away with the two bottles behind your seat and just keep changing the bottle on the bike frame at the aid stations. Most of the time it was Gatorade or something else I didn't use and I would just bring my own.

HELMET - You can't race without one, so just find one that is comfortable, fits you well, and meets all safety standards. Remember, if it's too loose, it will fall over your eyes when you lean forward into the profile position and that will drive you crazy. Also make sure it can be done up and undone easily.

SUNGLASSES - Often sunglasses are thought of as just making you look cool, but they are an absolute necessity when training or racing. And I don't really care if they cost $2.99 or $299. Just make sure you wear sunglasses to protect your eyes. Say you're going downhill at 40 mph. And the bee coming towards you is traveling 25 mph. when he hits your unprotected eye. That could be extremely serious! Always wear sunglasses and a helmet. Sun or not. I can think of at least 8 or 10 times over the years that something has hit my sunglasses hard enough to do lots of damage if my eyes had been unprotected. For those cloudy days, dark sunglasses will hamper your visibility. I always wore yellow tinted ones on those days and they brightened everything up considerably.

(22) RUN EQUIPMENT

There are several run equipment choices I feel can help you quite a lot in your quest for your first Ironman finisher medal.

SHOES - Of course well fitting shoes are a priority. I've tried every sort of shoe you can imagine over the years and have come to this conclusion:

You can train just as well and stay just as injury free in $50 shoes as you can in $150 dollar shoes. For instance, what if an outlet has a brand new 2004 model shoe on sale for $69, and sells the new, improved (same shoe) 2006 model for $149. Does that mean the older model is no good and will hurt your feet? Of course not! In order to stay competitive, manufacturers have to continually make small changes or improvements in their product to stay in step with the competition. The same as cars for instance.

The change from one year to the next may just be in the color, or new lacing system or a bit more build-up in some part of the shoe. Sometimes the change is really small.

Just shop around. See what's out there and in your training try several different types of shoes and when you find the one that fits perfect, feels great and never gives you blisters. then that should be your race day shoe.

Remember: Whatever you do, don't go out and buy some fancy shoe for race day because it looks really great. Go with the old shoe that got you there. Don't make any late changes.

I heard this story years ago and have never forgotten it and it is just a great example of what I'm talking about.

It's 1960, Rome Olympic Games. An African from Ethiopia shows up for the games. He is running in the marathon. He has no shoes. He didn't train in shoes. He trained back home by chasing rabbits for miles in his bare feet. A major shoe distributor at the games gave him a brand new pair of shoes to wear. He put them on. They hurt his feet. He took them off and said "No, thank you". He ran the marathon in bare feet. Twenty miles were over the cobblestones of Rome.

HE WON THE GOLD MEDAL!!

Now the shoe manufacturer really loves him and gives him shoes to train in at home.

Flash ahead four years to the next Olympic Games.

This African runner from Ethiopia shows up for the marathon once again. He is wearing shoes that he trained in at home. They don't hurt his feet now.

HE WON THE GOLD MEDAL!!

His name is Abibe Bikila.

The moral of the story is:

If he had worn the shoes for the 1960 Olympics, not only would he have not won gold, he would have trashed his feet. Just imagine the blisters. He wasn't accustomed to wearing shoes.

If he had not worn shoes in the 1964 Olympics, not only would he have not won gold, he still would have trashed his feet. He was not accustomed to bare feet anymore and his feet would not have the same toughness as the previous games.

So I repeat. Go with the footwear that you have done lots of training in. Don't make any late changes. When I found a pair of racing shoes I just loved, I wore them training until they were nicely broken in. I put those elastic, lock laces on them, so I never had to tie them again and I put them away. I wore them for 5 Ironman races. In that last transition, it was like putting on a favorite pair of slippers. I never had blisters from those shoes. I even ran one Ironman marathon in 3:34 in those old favorites. Oh, the cost of those shoes. Forty five dollars.

HEART MONITOR: A heart monitor is especially good for run training, because by its very nature it will help you avoid training too strenuously and as a result avoid injury. For proper use of a heart monitor see my comments on heart monitor training.

HAT: This may seem insignificant to some, but it can be extremely important on race day. This is especially so when most of you will be on the run course in the hottest part of the day. When you hydrate at the aid stations, you should also put cold water or ice in your cap in order to keep yourself as cool as possible.

SOCKS: Here is another item that people don't take too seriously, but now you can buy socks that are designed to help you avoid blisters. It's certainly something to look into.

FUEL BELT: I was so glad to see these hit the marketplace. The last thing you need is a big water bottle clunking against your side during an Ironman run. A fuel belt consists or 4 or 6 small bottles that are spread evenly around your waist. You hardly even know you have it on after a while.

(23) SOME THOUGHTS ON SWIMMING

If you are determined to attempt your first Ironman, but a bit
nervous about the swim, this may make you feel better.

Historically, more first time Ironman starters are more experienced in
running or biking. You are not alone!

I survived my first Ironman swim and so will you. When I watched those
crazy people back in 1982 and they were swimming 2.4 miles in the
ocean, my first thought was, "well I guess that rules me out".
Considering I could not swim a stroke at the time and had a healthy fear
of the water, my chances looked pretty slim.

Something happened though. The more I watched the race unfold, the
more I wanted to do it. By the time the T.V. version of Hawaii Ironman
1982 was done, I was determined to learn how to swim. I wanted to cross
that finish line.

Two years later, despite my earlier misgivings, I found myself knee
deep in the warm waters of Kona.

A cannon signaled the start and I was on my way. My first open water
swim! And what a swim it was. I had a really crappy stroke. I know that
now. I did not care at the time. I was in Kona. I was in the Ironman!

I got hit and kicked and run over, but luckily for me there were only around 1000 starters that day. It would get much worse in coming years as those numbers would grow to 2000 plus!

Back to Kona! It was surreal. Swimming out to the boat with the big orange sails that marked the turn. Watching tropical fish as I swam. Scuba divers sitting on the ocean floor waving as we swam by. Making the turn at halfway and an underwater photographer taking my picture as I rounded the boat and headed back. The amazing rush as I felt the current lift me and push me towards shore.

I can't even put into words what it felt like when I stood up after one hour and 38 minutes and realized I had finished the Hawaii Ironman swim. It was a defining moment in my life. I knew right then that before the day was done, I would be an Ironman. I had conquered my biggest demon.

I will never forget that transition tent. It was electric! It was like everyone was talking at once. You could "feel" the sense of accomplishment and relief in the air. Thinking back, I truly believe a lot of people in the race that year were dreading the swim.

I told you this story for a reason. It sure isn't to brag. It is meant to inspire you. It's to make you realize that if you want this bad enough, it's there for the taking. POWER! WISDOM! STRENGTH! You have that inside you. Now, let it out. Discover the abilities inside you that lay dormant, just waiting for an opportunity. You may just surprise yourself.

Don't make the same mistakes I did though. I pretty well did everything wrong when I tried to make myself a faster swimmer.

I read books. I swam thousands of lengths, reinforcing all my bad habits. I swam miles and miles with pull buoys, because my feet sank. I blasted my way through the water. It took me 10 years to take 15 minutes off my original Hawaii swim. The gun would go off and I would move my arms as fast I could for 2.4 miles.

It took years, but I soon discovered that I had to slow down in order to swim faster. I learned that swimming relaxed and using the natural buoyancy that we all have was the answer. It was not really how fast I got to the other end of the pool, it was how! I finally learned that 16 relaxed strokes every 25 meters is a ton better than 25 "move your arms as fast as you can" strokes.

I worked on that for the whole training season and when the next Ironman day arrived, I was determined to stay calm and relaxed. I used my new loooooong, smoooooth, stroke. Kept nice even balance on top of the water, and was very relaxed when I finished the swim. I thought, "well, I don't feel like I worked very hard or swam very fast, but if my time's slower that's ok, at least I feel great!"

My time that year was a personal best by five minutes! In one training season, by learning to relax, use proper technique and proper body balance, I made a huge improvement in my swimming.

Remember: It's not how many miles you swim in training. It's how you swim. That's the key.

A few other things..

If you don't manage to swim in the open water during your training, don't worry about it. Save it for race day like I did. The right swim technique will work anywhere. You should however, do some swimming in your wetsuit even if it's just in the pool. Just to get used to how it feels.

I highly recommend you do away with all those swimming aids. Kick boards and pull buoys should not really be part of your swim training. There's no need to learn how to be a great kicker. Swim with proper technique and kicking is not a big issue and you can save your legs for later in the day. If you learn proper balance in the water, your legs won't sink and you won't need to use pull buoys.

Don't feel you 'have' to join a swim club to improve your swimming. If you enjoy the club atmosphere, by all means, go for it. I always found I did better on my own.

Just remember this: The Ironman is an individual event. Much of it is done in solitude as you fight your own demons. Even if you have company in the marathon, they cannot carry you. It is what is inside YOU that will determine how your day ends.

(24) BIKE TRAINING AND OTHER STUFF

Hopefully I can give you a few bike training tips that will help you prepare for your first Ironman.

I'll repeat what I said in the bike equipment page. Be sure when you purchase a bike that it is the proper frame size for you. Also make sure that a professional gets you on the bike and "sets" it up for you.

In other words, if you really stretch at the bottom of the pedal stroke, the bike is not set up properly. If you are all scrunched up and are not extending your legs far enough, the bike is not set up properly. Something as simple as raising or lowering the seat can make a huge difference to your pedal stroke. Proper set up will ensure that you are making full use of the bigger leg muscles. Also, something as simple as having your bike set up properly will make your transition into the run a lot less painful.

When it comes to your actual bike training, many novice ironmen have the wrong idea. You don't have to go out and cycle hundreds and hundreds of miles. Maybe one day if you decide to really go for it and try and place in your age group you might want to look at more intense training. For your first attempt at an Ironman, you most likely will not be going out to set a course record for the bike leg. Ultimately, just crossing that finish line at the end of the day means you have accomplished something pretty special.

I would recommend doing one 7 or 8 hour ride about 8 weeks from your race weekend. Go out with a couple of people. Pack lots of food and water and plan to be gone for the day. Don't worry about how many miles. All you are doing is getting an idea of what it will be like to be on the bike for that long.

For the rest of the training year, try and bike 3 or 4 times a week. You can do 1 or 2 of those rides on a wind trainer or at a gym on one of their exercise bikes. As your season progresses, try and plan for one longer ride of 2 or 3 hours once a week. Again, don't worry about how many miles. Pay more attention to actual time on the bike and finding a cadence and speed that you're comfortable with. I strongly recommend heart monitor use on the bike. (Check the section on heart monitor training.) Try and stay at or below your target heart rate for most of your rides and your fitness level will continue to improve over time.

Be sure to try different fluid supplements and different types of solid nourishment until you find what agrees with you and then go with it. I would recommend getting used to one of the gels, because they are handy, packed with nourishment and likely can be found at most aid stations along the course. If not, they are small and easy to carry with you.

As your season progresses, you should try and do one transition ride every week. The best day for this is the day you're on your wind trainer. Ride for at least an hour and then run immediately after for at least half an hour. This will help you get used to the bike to run transition. It's not necessary to bike 4 or 5 hours and then run 15 miles in order to experience what it feels like. Trust me, after an hour on the bike, you will get the idea after about 4 strides into the run.

I won't kid you. There's nothing on earth that will *truly* prepare you for what you will experience when you leave the bike transition tent and head out on your first Ironman marathon. Get a feel for what this is like in the course of your training.

When you leave the bike behind and begin running, you will truly be looking into the eye of the tiger. It is here that you will begin to find out what you are made of.

On a lighter note, since biking is the topic, it's time to go back to Kona and tell you a bit about my first Ironman bike experience.

It's one hour before swim start. Someone said don't put air in your tires because they may burst overnight with the humidity as your bike sits in the transition zone.

So here I am, one hour before the start of the biggest race of my life, pumping up my rear tire. Being clever, I had put a brand new tube in the rear tire the night before. I pumped and pumped and just like a gunshot the tube exploded. Pretty well everyone within earshot looked and went oh-oh. I had failed to notice, but the tube had come right out of the tire and exploded. It was the wrong size!

No problem, I thought (sort of). I had brought along one spare in my infinite wisdom. I put it on. Of course, because I had bought it at the same time as the other one, it was also the wrong size. This time I saw it begin to bulge out of the tire. I did the only thing I could. I let air out until the tube went back into the tire. Most likely I had about 65-70 lbs of air pressure. About three quarters of what I actually should have used.

It's 4 hours later. Here I am on the King K. highway. The heat waves are massive. It's just over 100 degrees as the suns rays reflect off the lava fields. Every pedal stroke, I hear my rear tire squish into the soft asphalt. I have no spare left. My Ironman dream pretty well rests on that squishy tire. Each torrid mile merges into the next.

I feel alone. Nobody around me. Nobody cares about my own personal Hell.

Then, I see a vision.

A beautiful Hawaiian girl in a grass skirt and flowers in her long black hair about a hundred meters ahead. At first I think it's my heat fueled imagination. Perhaps a Hawaii hallucination.

BUT NO!

SHE'S REAL!

She's holding something out. My gorgeous savior. She has a sponge for me. A heavenly cool sponge to cool me. I straighten my helmet and glide

81

in towards her gracefully with all the élan of a world class cyclist, thinking, "I am Ironman!"

I would impress her to no end. Deftly swooping in toward her, I plucked the precious gift from her small hand and proceeded to **SMASH THAT GUAVA JELLY SANDWICH ON BROWN BREAD ALL OVER THE BACK OF MY NECK!**

By the way, if you're ever in Hawaii and get a chance to have lunch with a local, try a guava jelly sandwich, because they really, really pack it on.

Even to this day, I wonder what my angel in the grass skirt thought of the crazy Canadian guy on the bike. It sure looked like a sponge. Well, it was hot. Okay, so I was tired. Give me a break.

It was such a relief when I finally reached the bike to run transition. Words can't express how the first few dozen strides of the marathon felt, but at least now I was certain, the Ironman finish line was within my grasp.

I told you about my first Ironman bike experience for a reason.

Consider this. The furthest I ever biked in training was about 40 miles. I didn't really know how to train. I had no idea how far or how fast I should ride. I just went until I felt tired and turned around. I didn't really know what to eat or drink. As a matter of fact, until I began training for the race, I had not ridden a bike for about 20 years. In a nutshell, my bike training was pretty well non-existent.

On the actual day of the race, my bike was impossibly heavy. I had a rear tire that was missing about 40 pounds of air. I had no aero bars or clipless pedals.

Yet, my bike time was 7 hours and 39 minutes. That's all you need! If you can manage around an 8 hour bike split, you should have sufficient time to reach the finish line within the time limit.

My point is. If I could do that ride, under those circumstances, then I'm certain most of you reading this can as well.

Don't think for a moment you need hundreds and hundreds of miles of training. Don't be sucked into that.

Get yourself into overall good condition. Try and bike three or four times a week. Try and ride a bit longer as you get in better shape. Try one real long day about 8 weeks before the race. Get used to what you want to eat and drink for the race. Make sure your bike is set up properly. Do a bike to run transition at least once a week. Keep your bike properly maintained and clean.

Those are my bike training tips. If a coach puts you on a program and you are happy with it, then by all means go for it.

I'm just trying to convey that the spirit of the Ironman on race day will make you capable of more than you ever dreamed. Just being in the event, being cheered on, having prepared for this day and realizing your dream is within your grasp will more than compensate for any lack of ability or training.

(25) WHAT ABOUT THAT WIND TRAINER?

I remember the first time I brought a wind trainer home. It was meant as a bike training alternative when the weather was bad.

For 95% of my rides I would load my bike on the back of my car and drive out to the countryside where there was a wide shoulder and less traffic. Besides, there was no way on earth I would ever attempt to ride in the city. Far too dangerous and not very productive anyway. what's the point when you have to stop every few blocks for a traffic light.

As the years passed and the city grew, my favorite training routes became busier and busier. Almost every year a cyclist was getting killed or badly injured out on the highway. It seemed that every year that passed I was doing more and more training in my apartment, logging endless miles on the carpet highway.

Ultimately, something I never thought I would ever do finally happened. I did all my training indoors.

First of all let me say that I am notorious for trying radical training methods. My theory is...how can you know how something works unless you try it. For instance, I wanted to see how extreme distance training would help my marathon time. So for several months I kept ramping up my distance until I peaked at around 150 miles a week. In order to do that I ran about 24 hours a week. I did 2 a day training. So often, I would run 3 or 4 hours in the morning and then 1 or 2 hours in the evening. At one point I ran 25 days straight.

Was it worth it? Well I went to Las Vegas and ran their marathon in 3:03. It was a pretty good time, but I honestly felt that I would break 3 hours. Would I do it again? No. I think it's risky and just asking for an injury and the reward just wasn't there. However, it was in my nature to try. Besides, one day I will be able to tell my grandchildren that I ran 600 miles in one month.

Anyway, back to the wind trainer. My whole point of the run story was to explain my thought process. I was willing to try this radical bike training and give it a test in an Ironman because I was curious if it would really be that different. I'll let you be the judge.

I did *all* my training inside. 100%.

I used a program that slowly built up my distance to *five hours*. Or about two and a half movies that I watched while I cycled. I must say that there were many, many advantages to training at home.

1) Saved a lot of gas money.

2) Could come home from work, get on the bike and start training right away. No time lost to loading up the bike and driving for 25 minutes out and back.

3) My bike stayed real clean.

4) No potholes.

5) No dogs.

6) No cars.

7) No sudden rainstorms. Or in my part of the world -- snowstorms.

8) Great for transition training. Bike, jump off trainer, put on running shoes and be running 60 seconds later. Faster than an Ironman race day transition and great training for what it would feel like.

9) Ideal for interval training. You can gauge each interval exactly. Outside you're dealing with wind and uneven terrain, so each interval is different than the last.

10) You can get the same effect of climbing a big hill by doing low RPMs in a big gear.

11) Flat tire. Who cares? Sit on the couch and change it.

12) Nature calls? The bathroom's never far away.

DISADVANTAGES?

Sure.

1) If your bike is fancy, you don't get to show it off.

2) It can be boring (unless the movie is really good.)

3) You don't learn the small things like drinking and eating while you ride.

4) Seriously, I believe the biggest downside to not getting road miles in is that your bike handling skills will suffer. You could always try training on rollers, but that's an entirely different piece of equipment that takes a ton of practice to master. I don't really feel comfortable recommending them to those of you who are new to cycling.

Would I suggest you try just bike training inside?

Well, when I did the race, I was only around 15 minutes slower than I usually was. So really, in the big scheme of things, it didn't make any difference. I would do it again.

If you're living somewhere that is just not a good place for cyclists, then sure, don't obsess about it. Just get a good quality wind trainer and build yourself a program and go for it. Ultimately, I don't really think it will make that much of a difference come race day.

The one thing I would suggest is maybe in the last month or so of training when you're starting your taper for the big day, get outside and brush up on your bike handling skills. Six or eight rides should do it. They don't have to be real long. Thirty-forty kms. or so. That should get you ready.

You might think this whole idea is crazy, but I promised myself when I first considered writing a book for the novice Ironman triathlete that I would say what I thought and feel and not necessarily what you want to hear.

So you can take it or leave it. I'm just saying, don't give up on your dream because your area is not really made for cyclists. There is always a way.

By trying it myself and risking an Ironman race on it, I know you can do it if you choose to, with really very little difference in the final result.

(26) MORE ABOUT BIKING

No matter how hard you train for your first Ironman race, it won't necessarily guarantee that you will reach the finish line if you don't pay attention to details.

When it comes to your bike, there are mistakes that are made over and over again by triathletes new to the Ironman and hopefully I can point them out to you and help you realize your Ironman dream. Some of these mistakes I've made myself over the years, and I've had to learn the hard way.

Don't have your bike tuned up a few days before the big race. I would suggest 3 or 4 weeks would be the best time, so you can put in some mileage on it to make *sure* that everything is working the way it should. You don't want to be out on the bike course race day and find out the mechanic doesn't have the gears set properly and your chain comes flying off as soon as you stand up on the first hill. It happens. All you should really do the last few days is give your bike the best cleaning possible and make sure it's lubricated properly. If it's shifting o.k. and the brakes work fine, don't mess with it.

This goes for your fit on the bike as well. Race week is not the time to be adjusting your seat height or moving your handlebars. Go with the way it was set all through your training.

On average, the chances of getting a flat tire sometime race day is pretty slim. However, every race you will see people who *do* have flats. As much as it bugs you, take the time to learn how to the change a flat properly. Do it over and over again in your living room. Practice on the back tire. Don't worry about the front. If it's your first Ironman, and you're just trying to make the 17 hour cut-off, you don't want to be spending 30 minutes on that tire change. It could ultimately cost you reaching the finish line in time to be recorded as an official finisher. Every year there're people who miss the cut-off by minutes.

If you've trained for months and months and have come to rely on your bike computer for cadence, distance and speed etc., be SURE that your battery isn't going to quit on you 10 miles into the bike. I would spend the ten bucks and put in a new battery for the race.

Also, new battery or not, make sure the computer is working properly on your last bike ride when you get to the race venue. Sometimes traveling can knock the sensor out of alignment with the wheel and it won't work properly or not at all. This used to happen to me all the time when I traveled by car to the race and had my bike on a rack.

If your race is in a very humid, hot destination, I would suggest NOT pumping your tires up over 100 for the overnight stay in the bike transition area. Just put in 70 or 80, go to the start area early on race day and THEN pump the tires up to your race setting. If it's really humid, tires can expand overnight and burst if they're pumped up to the max. Don't worry about dragging a bike pump to transition. Without fail, every Ironman race I've ever done, the race organizers have plenty of pumps around and someone to help you. (Usually from the local bike shop.)

I would really suggest you have "two" spare tubes with you (or tires if you use sew-ups) for the race. If for no other reason, should you get a flat you don't want to spend the rest of the race in a panic that you have no spare left should you get a second flat. In other words, for your peace of mind, take two.

(27) DON'T EXPECT BIKE MAGIC

In preparing to take on the challenge of a first Ironman, I believe far too many athletes put too much emphasis on the bike they choose to purchase for the event.

Somewhere along the Ironman trail, many athletes have come to believe that the lighter, and more state of the art the bike, the faster they will finish the bike leg of the Ironman.

Nothing could be further from the truth. For example: You could put one athlete on a $10,000 bike and have him train without the aid of a proper diet or without paying attention to proper hydration choices and replacement drinks and the Ironman will spit him out like a cherry pit somewhere around mile 80 on the bike course.

Take another athlete and put him on a $800 reliable, average weight, used bike fitted with proper pedals and aero bars. Then have him pay particular attention all training year to proper diet, hydration, and race-day fueling techniques and somewhere around mile 80 of the same course he will call out "nice bike" as he passes athlete number one who is in for a very long, painful day.

Don't get all wrapped up in taking out a second mortgage so you can buy that "special" bike that is 6 ounces lighter than anything on the road. After all, you're going to be loading 5 pounds of water and food and gear on the thing before you even get out of transition. This is not your normal bike race. If you were just racing a bike century and that's it, then that might be a different story. But that's not the nature of this beast.

First of all you've most likely been bashed around for an hour or so in a wild free-for-all swim and for most of that time your heart-rate has been racing out of control. Plus, you still have a full marathon to consider after you get off the bike.

Your bike is just a small part of the Ironman equation. Don't get too wrapped up in light and fancy and expensive. I know, I've done that.

I had my best bike leg ever and my first thought was to fix up the old bike and keep racing it. However, I let my bike supplier talk me into buying a fancier, newer model that was so much lighter that I would go even faster. I never, never matched that bike ride over the next 10 years. Even on bikes valued 10 times more than my old standby. It was probably the biggest single mistake I made in my 20 year Ironman career. I should have gone with my very first instinct.

For some reason, a bike will just suit you. It suits your style, ability and "fits" you like that favorite pair of runners. When this happens, hang on to that bike. If you have to, save it mainly for races and get a second bike for the bulk of your training. It will last you for years that way.

I've raced on more than one high-end bike that I was just never comfortable on, no matter how light and fast they were supposed to be. At first it may seem cool to be the recipient of envious gazes from fellow triathletes when they see you on your bike the week leading up to the race. You are the bike "king".

Believe me, it's not so cool when these same athletes pass you out on the course with those dreaded words left in their wake. "Nice bike."

Every time you hear that, you will want to sink further and further into your bike seat. You will wish you were on a $250 beater. At least that way, you reason, you would have an excuse for getting passed over and over again. There is nowhere to hide out there.

To save yourself a ton of embarrassment and humiliation, be sure that your ability matches the bike you ride.

All my bikes are gone now, except for one. That same old bike is in my living room on a wind-trainer and if I decide to do this amazing race once again, when I turn 60, four years from now -- it will be on a very special, 16 year old bike.

(28) RUN TRAINING TIPS

The run training for your first Ironman should be approached with caution.

This is one area where you stand a good chance of being injured if you try and do too much too soon. If you are an accomplished runner with a few marathons under your belt, then most of this page isn't meant for you. I'm more concerned with those of you who don't really have a running background but still want your shot at the Ironman.

You will have to travel 26.2 miles on foot. Notice I said "travel" and not "run."

I imagine the list of first timers who have run the entire Ironman marathon distance from start to finish is very small.

Your goal should be to run more than you walk.

In my background I have run about 33 marathons, over 100 10-km races, 2 50-mile races, and have been in 14 Ironman Triathlons. I don't count the Ironman marathons in the 33 total because there is a world of difference between the two.

My fastest ever "marathon" is 2:54. My fastest ever Ironman marathon is 3:34. To do that I had to run "without stopping once" from the bike transition to the finish line.

It took me 15 years to get to that "without stopping once" stage.

So don't think you have to go out and run 100 miles a week to get ready for the Ironman. Don't even think you have to do a 20 mile run. It really isn't necessary.

Think in terms of "time on your feet" and not distance traveled.

I really wish I could convince every new triathlete to train with a heart monitor. Just by its very nature, a heart monitor will not let you run too fast too soon. It will help you stay injury free. It will make your running more enjoyable and it will motivate you when you can actually see your improvement as the months pass.

Reminder: When you use a heart monitor and train at or just below your pre- determined target, set a maximum of 90 minutes for those workouts. The "most" I ever did was 2 hours. What happens is, once you start getting into really good running shape, you start running quite a bit faster. So 90 minutes at a quick pace is enough. (Actually it's 60 minutes). The workout would consist of 15 minutes very slow to warm up. 60 minutes at or just below your target heart rate. Then a 15 minute very slow cool down, for a total workout of 90 minutes.

If you do longer runs, make them well below your target (20-25 beats) for the entire run. It will tend to creep up, but control it as best you can.

Sometime before your Ironman race, when you have trained yourself into really good running shape, try an extended outing. Make sure it's a good 8 weeks or so before the big day. Try and convince someone to come along with you on their mountain bike. That way they can carry extra water for you.

Say you plan it for a Sunday. Make Saturday your rest day and plan for 3 or 4 hour run on Sunday. Most first time ironmen are on the marathon course somewhere between 4 and a half and 7 hours. What you want to do is try and do your long training run so it emulates your upcoming Ironman run.

In other words, don't bother trying to run the whole thing. Run without stopping for the first 60-90 minutes. This will start to make you a bit tired. Take a two minute break and walk. From there run 10-12 minutes and then walk 2 minutes. Keep doing that until your 3 and half to 4 hour run is finished. If you could work 2 or 3 of these into your training that would be great, but do at least one for sure.

What you have done is practice what it will be like to run between the aid stations and then walk through them. Take what you feel you need for food and water and you are on your way to the next aid station. If you plan and train for this, then you won't be disappointed if you go out expecting to blast your way through the entire marathon course. It just won't happen.

By having a plan, you will have a ballpark time of how long it will take you to cover 26 miles. This is really important because you have to BE aware of the time remaining before the official cut off. Don't go into the last five miles or so with time running out. You want to have a bit of a cushion so you can enjoy the final few miles.

KONA-1984 (first Ironman)

Thank God I'm off that bike! I'm just so amazed that the squishy tire made it through 112 miles without letting me down.

It's hard to describe the first few running?? strides coming out of the bike transition. I just knew this was going to be "really" challenging.

I had visions of running through that whole marathon course, but that was soon a distant memory. It seemed to take forever to get out of Kona and onto the highway. That's where most people started walking. It seemed like the longer you walk, the harder it is to get started again. I really tried to get into a run and walk pattern and it seemed to help. I wouldn't let myself walk for too long at one time without running, even if it was barely a fast walk.

As day passed and turned to dusk and then darkness, the King K. highway was alive with litesticks. It really was an amazing sight. It was very moving to see people so determined to get it done. One way or the other.

95

A volunteer's encouragement to "keep going" became so important.

Periodically an ambulance would scream by and an iron dream would be shattered. I hope they tried again. It really was heartbreaking to see someone taken off the course after coming so far.

With ten miles to go and a look at my watch, I knew with a certainty that this day I would be an Ironman. Believe me, every mile closer your heart beats a little bit faster. The excitement builds.

Now the lights of Kona are clearly visible.

The dream called "Ironman" is near. The same dream that awaits you.

(29) PROS AND CONS OF GROUP TRAINING

I've had lots of triathletes ask me about the benefits of training with a group as opposed to training alone.

I've tried both and this is what I've concluded based on years of hit or miss training.

In the beginning (back in 1983) most of us had no idea at all how to even begin to train for the Ironman. It was just too new.

Everybody kind of went off on their own and trained at their own speed.

As the Ironman developed and continued to grow, so did the opportunities to get in on group training.

Now you can train for the entire year in some sort of group right up until the actual race. I found that groups have their place, but only up to a point.

It's a good way to learn some of the basics. Especially in swimming and cycling. For others it's a social event when they get out and train with others. Ultimately having a coach does not guarantee the desired race result. Regardless of who you train with or how much coaching you have, how your Ironman race turns out will depend on your motivation, determination and strength of character more than anything else.

Here's what happened to me one year.

For years I struggled with my swimming and finally decided that I would spend the whole training year with a swim group. Three nights a week. I never missed a night. I had to park about half a mile from the pool. It was one of the coldest winters in years. For weeks I would freeze on the way back to my car after swimming. I never disliked any training experience more in my entire 25 year career, but stuck with it because I was determined to improve.

Finally race day came and after all that, I was 2 minutes slower than the year before when I trained alone.

That was 15 years ago and I have not trained with a group since.

Looking back, I'm pretty sure of what went wrong. For one thing, the training was far too competitive. They had slow lanes and medium lanes and fast lanes and everyone was trying not to get left behind. All attempts at proper technique soon went out the window. Often these group coaches concentrate too much on all the strokes. I wasted a lot of time on butterfly and backstroke and kick boards etc.

I realize now that all you have to do is learn the smoothest, most economical front crawl that you possibly can. Doing hundreds of meters of kicking with a board is a complete waste of time for a triathlete. If you want coaching, it makes more sense to pay for some private (one on one) coaching for a few weeks and then take what you learned and train on your own.

As far as biking goes, once you learn the proper technique, it's time to hit the road on your own. Use a group or class or a few group rides to learn the basics, but I wouldn't recommend spending the whole year training with a group.

In the Ironman, it will be you and the course. It's extremely important to get the feel of being out on the road battling a headwind on your own. Cycling with a group and having just 2 other cyclists in front of you can cut the headwind by a huge amount. That's exactly why you can't draft in the race. It's a serious unfair advantage to draft. Group riding just is not a great way to prepare for this race. It is good however, for learning to ride with others around you. I would not really recommend spending the entire training year cycling with a group.

Some other disadvantages of group training:

You end up training on their schedule instead of yours. You constantly have to fit in that time no matter what.

There will be times that you are tired and not really prepared to train at the group's fast speed, but you really have no choice. One session you may feel great and they will train too slow for you. It can work both ways.

There is also the added expense of club fees or group swimming programs.

Some people get far to competitive in group training. That should be saved for the race.

Ultimately, every athlete must make their own choice. I suppose some need a group for motivation. Or as I said before, it may be an important social part of their life. So it seems there are some good points to both methods of training, so my advice is this:

Use the best of both worlds. Use group training to get started and learn technique etc., but also do a significant portion of your training on your own. Possibly pick one day a week where you run with a big group and make it your social run. Plan a long ride with a group of friends and make it a social, easy ride.

Do the bulk of your training and the more intense training on your own, and I believe you will have your best possible result come race day.

(30) OVERTRAINING

This is a statement I read recently. "Remember that when you are not training, someone out there is and you will lose to that person when you meet on race day."

This statement was directed towards highly competitive athletes, but just the same, by its very nature, this reasoning can lead to injury.

I really believe that regardless of whether you are a pro triathlete or first time Ironman, this is not the best thought process to follow.

To me it makes more sense to worry less about the other person and concentrate on the training regimen that's best for you. Being afraid to miss a training day because someone else might get a step ahead of you is a recipe for disaster. All athletes have different physical tolerance levels and must progress within their capabilities and not push themselves when they obviously need rest.

Often an Olympic athlete, like a swimmer for example, will suffer an injury and be forced to take 4 or 5 weeks off from serious training. Then soon after being back from injury, they enter a competition and have some of the best results of their career. You see it with pro athletes as well. A hockey player misses a week or two of playing and when he returns to the ice he has a career night.

To me there's a simple explanation. They were forced into giving their body a long period of rest that was obviously needed. Chances are they were overtraining before their forced layoff. Their bodies welcomed the rest and responded with amazing results.

Over the years I've had times when I've pushed my body to the limit just to see what I could do and if it would improve my race results. I was capable of enormous training regimens, but ultimately found that training more didn't necessarily result in better race results. More often then not it resulted in injury.

For example: The scenario I explained earlier about running extreme distances in training to see what it would do for my marathon time. Over a 5 month period I kept increasing my weekly distance. I maxed out at 155 miles a week.

The last month of training before I had intended to taper was a monster. The weeks went 140 miles, 145 miles, 150 miles and 155 miles or almost 600 miles in a month plus working a full-time job. It was during the last week and a half that I started to feel soreness in my heels. Like many other odd aches and pains I developed over the years, I just trained right through it assuming it would go away. Well it didn't. It became so bad that I had to go to a doctor and was diagnosed with plantar fasciitis. It was an extremely serious case and cost me the marathon I was training for, and even an Ironman race 5 months later.

I did mention to two different coaches that my heels hurt and it felt like they were bruised. They had no idea what it was. When I told my doctor the same thing a week or so later he knew right away what the problem was. He diagnosed plantar fasciitis immediately. Ironically, when I looked it up on the Internet later, it said that the first sign of plantar fasciitis is a feeling not unlike having bruised heels. It taught me an important lesson. A coach is not a doctor. If you are injured, go to a doctor.

Despite having my heel injected with an anti-inflammatory before the Ironman I had to drop out 5 miles into the run. It was a devastating injury and I never allowed myself to overtrain again.

It really messed up an entire year.

My suggestion to anyone training for the Ironman is to listen to your body. It's true that often you will get numerous aches and pains and twinges that come and go as you put your body through the rigors of training for a distance event. If you quit training every time something ached, you would never train.

The best way I found to approach these nagging aches and pains is monitor them "very closely." Say for example your heel begins to hurt like mine did. The first time you notice the pain do one more running workout. If it's still there, stop running and concentrate on your swimming and biking. That's the beauty of the Ironman. Often an injury will allow you to do at least one of the other disciplines.

See your doctor right away and tell him your concerns. He may refer you to physiotherapy. Had I done this it may have saved my entire year. Plantar fasciitis would have been diagnosed right away. A program of stretching 3 times a day and maybe some shoe inserts and I could have avoided the injury becoming chronic. At most I would have lost one or two weeks instead of the entire season.

So I believe that's the key to avoiding serious injury. If it's a normal ache or pain it will disappear in a few days. If it persists through several training days, stop and get it diagnosed.

Pushing too hard in your training can cause other problems as well. You can just simply run out of energy and every workout becomes difficult. It's times like this that training is just no fun. If you go out on a training run or bike and just know you have nothing in the tank, stop and go home. Take two or three days off completely and do things that have nothing to do with swim, bike, run. Above all, avoid the mind set that you will lose all the conditioning you worked so hard for if you take extra time off. It just won't happen.

Give your body a break. When you return to training, you'll most likely feel revitalized and begin to enjoy training once again.

Strange as it may sound, my best competition year was when I decided to take extra days off whenever I felt drained. It was a complete about face from all the years that I just pushed through the fatigue. Training tired all the time often means you will eventually run out of gas somewhere on the Ironman course.

Remember:

Listen to your body.

Take a few days' extra rest if you feel tired all the time.

If a pain persists through a few training days, stop, see a doctor and concentrate on the events that don't aggravate the injured area.

Don't worry about how everyone else is training. Do what works for you.

(31) A TYPICAL TRAINING WEEK

My intention is not to set up a training week program for you. Instead I would just like to suggest a few guidelines that may make your preparation for your first Ironman a bit easier.

As a rule, your training week will most likely total anywhere from 12-16 hours.

A lot depends on which of the disciplines you may already be quite skilled at and which need a lot of work. It also depends if you decide to incorporate strength training into your program. (I highly recommend at least lower body training-squats). Don't forget, you will only be spending 30 minutes or so in the weight room per session.

If you are not a swimmer, then I would suggest at least 4 and possibly 5 days of swimming per week. It will pay you HUGE dividends if you have a smooth, energy saving stroke come race day.

If you are a runner, you would probably get by with 3 running days a week and spend more time on the other elements.

A normal week might consist of 4 swims, 3 runs, 3 bikes and at least 2 and preferably 3 weight sessions.

Whenever possible try and do two disciplines per day. With the exception of a long run day or long bike day -- 2 hours or more. In that case only do the one event.

Be sure to have one day per week with no physical stress. You can use your rest day for a visit to the chiropractor, massage therapy or just to relax and maybe do some visualization about your upcoming race.

Be sure to have your rest day the day *before* you have a long bike or run planned. Also make sure the day after is an easier day. For instance weight training and a swim.

I found with swimming that an hour in the pool was usually sufficient.

It's really important to get used to the bike/run transition. So I would suggest that once a week for sure you bike at least an hour (exercise bike or wind-trainer is fine) followed within 3-4 minutes at the most by a run of at least 30 minutes. This will give you a good idea how the different muscles react to that transition. This is a very key part of your training week.

There will be times when you just feel totally worn out after weeks of steady training. When that happens take a full weekend off and do nothing at all connected with your Ironman training. When Monday arrives you'll be all set to get back at it.

After a few months it would also be a good idea to just have an easy week. Maybe do just one maintenance work-out per day for 6 days, have your full day off and then go back to your regular training program.

Often potential ironmen forget how important rest is. It's a vital component of your preparation. Training 25 days straight without let-up will not guarantee a successful race. I know, I've tried it. If anything it could lead to injury.

If anything out of the ordinary starts to hurt and it's a pain you've never felt before -- stop what you're doing!! Rest and then try again. For instance, if you feel something in your knee while running that could potentially be an injury surfacing, don't keep running on it. Swim for a few days because it's non impact and won't stress cause additional stress. Rest your knee and then try a short run and see what happens. If it feels fine, then don't worry about it. Just monitor it for the next few runs. If it persists, have it checked out.

It's important to keep your training week as consistent as possible, but not when it might lead to serious injury. Just take a step back and look after it before you carry on with your program.

Early in my career, I was injured several times because I insisted on training through pain and made a bad situation worse. Don't fall into that trap.

Most of all, enjoy your training. In the process of getting ready for your first Ironman, you're also getting yourself into possibly the best shape of your life.

Work out a plan that fits your lifestyle, watch your diet, use a heart monitor, use proper fluid and food replacements while training, have proper rest, and you will go into your first Ironman well prepared.

(32) VISUALIZATION AND TRAINING

Ask most triathletes and they will tell you they have never used visualization as tool for their triathon training. In fact, they most likely have little idea what it's about. It's surprising considering that world class athletes have used visualization to enhance their training and race performance for many years.

You may well have watched athletes in action without realizing they were using a form of visualization at that very moment. For example, have you ever watched a high jumper in the Olympic Games? Before they make their approach to the bar, they have already visualized the entire jump in their mind. It's the very same with world class divers. Before they ever leave the board or platform they visualize the dive to reinforce in their memory, every intricate aspect of that dive.

I remember reading an interview of Canadian figure skating champion Elizabeth Manley after the 1988 Winter Olympics. She stated that a big part of her training was lying down, relaxing and visualizing her entire long program in her mind. Often she would get to a very difficult spot in the program and see herself falling. She would start over and do it again and again until one day she visualized a perfect performance. It was that day that she knew she was ready to perform it on the ice. She skated a flawless long program during the Olympic Games and won a silver medal and it was close to being gold.

Visualization can easily be incorporated into your Ironman training.

I found that once I learned the proper way to swim -- with a long, smooth, stroke -- that visualization was instrumental in imprinting that stroke into my memory. You can do it as well. On those days when you just need a physical break or the weather is just plain lousy, give this a try.

Find a quiet place and relax and imagine yourself at your race start line. Go over exactly how you want the swim to unfold. Where you want to be when the gun goes off. Visualize the long, smooth, relaxed stroke you plan to use and even how you intend to make your transition from swim to bike. You can visualize your entire race, so come race day, nothing is left to chance. You can even visualize something going wrong. For instance, a flat tire. You can visualize yourself relaxing and just taking it in stride. Envision yourself staying calm and doing what has to be done so you can carry on with your race.

Visualization is just a great training tool that I would recommend you incorporate into your training program.

When you're visualizing your race, don't forget to imagine yourself in that last 50 feet to the finish line and how it will feel to complete your first Ironman.

(33) SHOULD YOU HAVE A SPONSOR?

Having a race sponsor for your first Ironman Triathlon can seem like a pretty good idea. Taking part in an Ironman has become a pretty expensive affair these days and it's always nice to have help along the way.

Especially with things like expensive bike equipment, lodging, and travel expenses etc.

After all, you may only be required to wear their name on your race clothing. It seems like a small price to pay to have yourself a sponsor.

Few people realize the responsibility that seemingly comes along with wearing a sponsor's name.

It can often become a trying proposition for many athletes.

I know because I've been in that situation. It's amazing the amount of extra pressure you can put on yourself by having a sponsorship. It was always on the back of my mind that I had to do really well to justify any financial aid I had received.

Along with everything else there is to worry about during an Ironman, there was always this nagging feeling that I didn't want to let my sponsor down. Not to mention that I didn't want to fail and embarrass myself by having to face my sponsor and tell him that I didn't finish the race for some reason.

It's quite amazing the things that go through your mind.

I really feel that for your first Ironman you have enough to worry about. In hindsight, it makes sense to me now that having a race sponsor for your first Ironman attempt is not a really great idea. The last thing you need is the added pressure of trying to justify what a sponsor has done for you.

My suggestion is to try and forgo sponsorship when attempting your first Ironman. See how it goes and if you decide down the road to continue on with an Ironman career, perhaps then, it would make more sense.

Whatever you decide, make sure you fully understand what you're getting yourself into when you accept the responsibility that comes with your decision.

(34) THOUGHTS FROM THE PROS

Often a pro Ironman will have insights into the Ironman Triathlon that come from years of competing at the highest level. Here are just a few written comments from some of the most accomplished triathletes the sport has ever seen.

DAVE SCOTT -- "If you experience a disappointment at a race, don't make too much of it. The worst thing you can possibly do is judge yourself too harshly, because it takes a long time to restore broken confidence. You would be better off congratulating someone who had an excellent race that day: It acknowledges that both of you did as well as you could."

MARK ALLEN -- "It's normal to have fear. It keeps us from doing stupid things. But it can also hold us back from having an incredible experience. My fears -- about Ironman, marriage, having a child -- could have kept me from giving 100 percent of what I had to give. If I had given into my fears, even a little bit, I would not have won that race six times."

JULIE MOSS (ALLEN) -- "Fear, all kinds of fear, lurks in inaction: fear of getting started, fear of failure, fear of never being able to get in shape, fear of not knowing how to make a goal happen, fear of how bad it might hurt. The only way to face fears, to transform them, is to get out there and take the first steps.

SCOTT TINLEY -- "You ever wonder what regular people think when they hear that close to 20,000 people are trying to get an entry into Kona? They're thinking all those people must have a screw loose, that's what. Yet, I'd bet 1,000 sit-ups that more than a few of them dream about crossing the finish line, all tan and trim, the crowd screaming, their toothpaste commercial smiles caught and beamed out over the airwaves. And I bet that when they wake up in the morning, more than a few roll over and try to hide from the gnawing desire that they, too, could have that same screw loose.

Maybe they are realizing that too many of us die too young or too late. Maybe they know that we pull ourselves up by making money, making the grade; all the while taking less and less time to face the fact that there are some things in life we need to do. Just because.

I think the Ironman is one of those things. For all those people, I can't pretend to know why. Hell, I barely have an idea why I did close to 50 of them myself. But I know people are changed by an Ironman. Ironman finishers leave a mark on the world.

Try to define that. Go ahead. The words will never come. It is enough to hear the stories, to watch the returning smiles. Witness the metamorphosis.

Yeah, there is a price--relationships, jobs, sunburns, missing toenails; there always is for the good stuff. But the call of the distant drum is too loud to ignore, too powerful to pawn off as some mid life crisis of the middle manager or desperate plea of a soccer mom. All they want is their one day. One day full of enough feeling and emotion to last an eternity.

But like war, marriage, tight jeans and stick shift cars, the Ironman isn't for everybody. As much as it can give, it can take. If it were easy, it wouldn't mean the same. Even dreams are fair game in the forecast of one's decisions.

I know there are ways to validate one's life. There has to be. The Pulitzer Prize winning author Katherine Anne Porter once said that salvation can only be found through religion and art. I believe that great feats of physical endurance include both those traits.

And in a world that tries its hardest to separate us from what matters, the ironman helps us to reconnect with the pulse of our lives. As long as it does that, we will be happy to have made the decision to even attempt the dream."

(35) WHAT WILL YOUR FINISH TIME BE?

Your first Ironman and your projected finish time often becomes
a frequently asked question.

What do you think your finish time will be? This question will come from
friends, family, co-workers and fellow athletes.

It's amazing just how loaded this question is.

What should you say?

Realistically, there are three possible finish time scenarios.

The first is the "I don't care as long as I finish under the deadline." You
tell this one to just about everyone who asks.

The second is the time you tell to very few people, or possibly nobody at
all. It's the time you have calculated in your mind that you think you will
actually do the race in. You've taken the swim time you know you can do,
your best bike time you think you are capable of and added about an hour
to your best individual marathon race time. Then you've probably added
on 5 minutes for each transition.

So for example: You figure you can smash out that swim in 60 minutes.
You know from your training that you can handle that 112 mile bike ride in
6:45. Plus no sweat for the marathon in 4:15, because after all, you've

run a marathon in just over 3 hours. Plus 10 minutes for transitions. You feel strongly that your finish time will quite possibly be very near 12:15 - 12:30.

Then there is the third scenario. It's the finish time that your Ironman probably will be.

Ninety per cent of the time, a first time Ironman will have a finish time between what they tell everyone and what they truly believe they are capable of.

In the above scenario, I would project that the athlete's time would be somewhere in between 13:30 and 14 hours.

This is because they imagine themselves running the entire marathon. They just believe they will run it slower than normal. In reality, only a handful of first timers will *ever* run their first Ironman marathon from start to finish. Or, for that matter, even run 75% of the marathon.

Unless you've been there, it's hard to factor in how much an energy wasting swim will cost you. The weather is almost always a factor that is seldom included in the equation. Through excess adrenalin, wasted energy, heat or cold, the average first-time ironman will be shocked at just how bad legs can feel when the bike is left behind and you head out onto the marathon course.

As a result, the marathon will be the great equalizer and even if the above athlete did the one hour swim and 6:45 bike and rolled through the transitions in 5 minutes each, the marathon time will go into the tank the minute the walking begins. Once you start the 15-16 minute miles the time piles up pretty quickly.

This is the reality of the Ironman Triathlon.

The best thing to do, is to go in with a completely open mind. If you have never been there, then don't even try and guess or estimate what your finish time should be. In the big scheme of things, it just is not that important. Crossing that finish line and having the word "Ironman" in front of your name certainly is.

So when you are asked that "what do you think your finish time will be" question, just tell the truth.

Just say you really don't know, because believe me, until you've been there, you really don't.

(36) FINDING A PLACE TO STAY

Picking the right accommodations for your race can have a positive impact on your Ironman experience. Here are five important tips to consider when choosing that all important place to stay.

(1) Be sure to book early. The longer you wait to book, the fewer options you leave yourself. Often rooms are booked a year ahead of time. Athletes who know there is a good chance they may return to the same race the next year, will re-reserve a room before they leave town. Even if you're not entirely positive you'll be ready to race the following year, book anyway. Even if a deposit is required, it's normally 100% refundable if you give them fair notice. It's not usually a problem at an Ironman venue, because they know there will always be someone else to take the room.

(2) Location, location, location. This is very important. You want to try and get just the right distance away from the race start and transition area. Often there will be a hotel listed as the race headquarters. Most likely that's where registration will take place and at most IM races, this hotel will be right beside the race start area. You definitely should try avoid staying at that location for a few reasons. First of all, it will be expensive. It will also be very, very busy. It's simply too close to the action and hype. By the same token, don't book so late that you end up staying outside of town. It's just not convenient for registering, the expo, and carbo and awards dinners. Also, you don't want a drive so far, that you have to worry about car problems causing you to be late getting to the race start. Don't leave anything to chance. I would say the perfect distance would be about

a 15-20 minute walk. That would make it about an 8 minute bike ride or around 5 minutes by car if you're driving. That way you're close to everything, but still have a bit of buffer zone from all the hype.

(3) Remember that by going to the host IM website for accommodation information, you will most likely only be given a few options. Often they will give you a list of expensive hotels and if at all possible you should try and avoid staying in a hotel room. A better option is to key the name of the race venue into Google. For instance "Penticton accommodations" if you're going to Ironman Canada. Or "Kona accommodations" if you're going to Hawaii. This should bring up a better variety of available accommodations with contact information etc. The best method I ever came up with personally was to phone the chamber of commerce of the particular city (pretty well every town or city has one). You'll get a real live person who actually lives in the area and you can tell them exactly what you're looking for. They will also have all the phone numbers for you.

(4) Find a motel with full kitchen facilities. Avoid hotel rooms unless it's your only option. A fully equipped kitchenette will have a stove, fridge and all the dishes, pots and pans and utensils. It's absolutely the best way to go for an Ironman competition. Also, they are often less expensive than the fancy hotels. With a kitchenette unit, you can just go shopping at the nearest supermarket when you arrive and basically be able to stay with the diet you are used to. Personally, I think it's a far better and safer option than eating restaurant food three times a day. You just never know for sure what you're eating. Also, you have a refrigerator to keep your drinks cool and in between meal snacks fresh. It really is the very best option.

(5) Try and make sure you are not right on the Ironman course. This can make it difficult to return to your lodging after the race. For the most part the roads will be closed until the last few entrants have reached the finish. try and be at least 2 or 3 blocks either side of the main course. When you arrive at your choice of lodging, be sure to take practice drives (if you have a car there) down to the main transition area. Decide ahead of time where you plan to park on race morning. Once again, stay away from the main course as you may find that you can't get out after the race. Leave for the check-in and numbering on race morning as early as possible. The prime parking spots will be gone very early. If you're in short walking

distance, (15-20 minutes) you have nothing to worry about. Try and avoid walking to much further than that, as you will have your bike and all your gear to haul after the race. It would be ideal if you had someone to help you out after the race.

Ultimately, planning ahead will make your race experience all that much better. Make the choices that will make your stay stress free and enable you to concentrate on the race itself.

(37) RACE WEEK. IT'S HERE!

It's really here. It's race week and the countdown to your first Ironman.

Hopefully, you have found that ideal place to call home for Ironman week. I would always try and arrive about five or six days before the race. Normally arriving sometime Wednesday afternoon and leaving the Tuesday after the race. Often the race will be on a Sunday with the awards on the Monday night.

Normally things really start to get rolling on the Wednesday before a Sunday Ironman. People from all over the world start to arrive. It's pretty exciting.

This is a typical schedule:

Wed. - Merchandise tent normally opens

Thur. - This is normally the day the "Iron fair" or expo opens. Sometimes there are seminars you can attend.

Fri. - This is your registration day and bike check day. Also it's when carbo load dinner will be if it's a Sunday race. (As far as I know, pretty well every Ironman race is on a Sunday).

Sat. - For special cases this is a late registration day. Usually there is a mandatory meeting. This is important. Go to it. Sometime in the afternoon you will do your check in. Say goodbye to your bike. Also, bring t-shirts to exchange. Find the Japanese. They bring tons of brand new t-shirts and are great traders.

Sun. - OMG!

This is important and concerns training on race week.

Do your last fairly hard workout on Tuesday.

Wednesday is a very easy day. I usually arrived on Wednesday so after I checked into my motel, I would go for a very easy 30 minute run to wind down after traveling.

Thursday is a good swim day. Try and avoid swimming the whole course. Also, avoid any long bike rides from here until the race. They serve no good purpose. Don't plan a run for this day.

Friday is a complete rest day. Walk around the town. The store owners and people you see on the street may well be your race day volunteers. Be friendly towards them.

Sat. - Many use this for a complete rest day, but really should not. Do a bit of a run and a bit of a swim. (15-20 minutes). Your bike will most likely be checked in unless you are doing a late check-in. I was usually driving so I would take two bikes to the Ironman. Just so I could ride 20 minutes or so on Saturday. By doing this on Saturday you're increasing your circulation and keeping your muscles loose for Sunday. The run and swim will do nicely for this if you can't bike. Doing a short workout on Saturday is a very important part of your race week preparation.

I got in the habit of having my last meal on Saturday *finished* by 4 P.M. I always had a kitchenette. Normally I had salad and pasta. Eating anything new to you is not recommended. Stay with what got you this far. Eat as you would at home after a long training day.

When you checked in your bike you should not have left your water bottles with your bike. No need to. Take them race morning. Remember that you can go to your bike and transition bags on race morning. Get all your mixtures (drink supplements) done on Saturday night and put them in the refrigerator. Get all your swim gear laid out. You take that with you on race morning. Wear some old sweats over your tri suit or swimsuit. Wear a loose top.

YOU WILL HAVE TO REMOVE THESE TO GET ALL YOUR RACE
NUMBERS PUT ON!

If you have a backpack you can fold up and make quite small, it will be a
great help to you after the race. You will have your bike and all your gear
to carry out and a backpack will free up your hands. Don't bother hauling a
bike pump down to transition. There will be lots there. The bike support
people will be in transition race morning to help you out with air or last
minute problems.

When you leave your accommodation for the last time Sunday A.M. to go
to transition, you should have the full water bottles to put on your bike.
You should also have any water bottles and gear placed in the appropriate
marked special needs bags (one for bike, and one for run). When you go
down to the transition area there will be a designated spot to drop off each
bag. If you are using a fuel belt for the run, have it prepared Saturday
night as well. Take it to the start area and put it in your "run" transition
bag with your running shoes gear.

Also take all the food you plan to use for race day. Put it on your bike or
in the appropriate transition bag.

Don't forget your wetsuit, goggles, swim cap and timing tag. Usually you
are given your cap, timing tag and ID bracelet at registration. Your ID tag
gets you into the carbo-load and the awards dinners and stays on until you
leave for home or maybe for weeks after until you finally cut it off.

Put your swim stuff (goggles, cap, wetsuit) in your dry-strip bag that they
will give you with the rest of your bags during registration. When you
finally decide to put your wetsuit on, put your old sweats and old runners
and lucky bear or picture of your loved one or lucky trinket into that same
bag and toss it in the pile with the other 2000 bags. Somehow it will
magically appear with your other transition bags after the race. If you are
really smart and paying attention, you will also be folding up an empty
backpack as small as you can and sticking it in that same bag as well
before it goes on the pile. You will be glad you did. You will also be really
glad you're not hauling around an unnecessary bike pump after the race.

AND FINALLY---WHEN THE HECK DO I GET UP ON RACE MORNING AND WHAT THE HECK DO I EAT AND DRINK?

Those are two very good questions and important ones to round out your race preparations.

Are you ready for this?

Get up at 3:30 A.M.

You're tossing and turning anyway. You're also worried about sleeping in. Ask the motel or hotel for a wake up call at 4 A.M. just to be on the safe side.

Eat first thing and then don't eat again until you are on your bike! I learned this from lots of experimenting over 14 Ironman race mornings.

You should have spent Thursday to Saturday hydrating. When your urine is clear and copious you are properly hydrated. That will most likely be sometime Saturday.

Trust me on this. Eating too much too close to the race can only result in digestive problems you don't really need.

Don't drink lots on race morning. Sip on one water bottle if it makes you feel better. Don't forget, you are already hydrated. You don't want a bunch of food or water sloshing around during the swim. It serves no good purpose.

This is what I ate and also what Dave Scott sometimes ate for breakfast.

2 pieces of whole wheat toast, and one or two bananas. That's it. I usually had a cup of tea with it. No milk and a couple of sweeteners. Keep the toast lightly buttered or dry.

I had a long shower.

Transition opens at 5 A.M. Be there at 5 A.M. or 5 or 10 minutes after. No later. Be one of the first to get number marked. You will have no long lineups at the porta potties. You will have time to reflect. You will not have to rush to do anything. You will get a great parking spot. Park as close as possible to the transition area, being sure that you are not too close to the race course. As I said earlier, you want to be able to get back to your room after the race. I really believe being early is the BEST system. This is one of the greatest times of your life. Take it all in.

Now the time has come. The question you were asked the moment you were Ironstruck.

"COME, COME SHOW US WHAT YOU ARE MADE OF."

That time is here. Good luck and Godspeed!

(38) RACE WEEK MISTAKES TO AVOID

Often mistakes are made during race week that can have significant impact on race results.

For an event like the Ironman, training is done over many months and possibly an entire year. Endurance is built up over a long period.

There is nothing you can do in the week leading up to the Ironman that is going to increase your endurance.(Apart from resting.)

Yet it never fails. Every Ironman I've ever been to you see people out on their bikes hammering out a 70 mile ride 3 days before the race. Or else they're out doing a 12 mile run in the blazing heat! Go figure.

Or there are some who will go out and swim the entire course about 3 times that final week.

All they're doing is burning valuable energy that cannot be replaced before the race. It would make more sense to just lie on the couch that last 7 days. They would be further ahead.

If you are not physically ready for the race when you roll into town, there is nothing that will save you in that last week.

There are plenty of ways to taper before the big race. How about Kim Bushong's famous "TV Taper." He claimed he sat around for three weeks prior to Ironman '82 and watched TV and ate chocolate bars. He led for the entire bike leg and wasn't caught until 10 miles into the run.

Though this is not recommended for everyone, it worked for him.

I would suggest that with 3 weeks to go, you do not increase intensity or distance of training. Decrease the actual time you spend training, but keep the intensity level normal.

I wouldn't recommend doing any weight workouts within 10 days of the big race.

If your race is on Sunday, your last hard work-out of any type would be on Tuesday. Remember, no long distances at this point. Wednesday and Thursday are recovery days from your last work-out on Tuesday. No high intensity or distance of any type. Maybe an easy early morning swim before breakfast or perhaps a easy 30 minute run.

Yes, I realize I'm repeating myself in these two paragraphs, but they are important and bear repeating.

Remember, Friday is your complete rest day (not Saturday as many people tend to believe). No biking, running or swimming. Stay out of the sun. Find some shade and read this book.

Saturday, the day before the race, spend 15-20 minutes on each event. No more. This will loosen muscles, increase circulation and help shed any excess water retained from a few days of inactivity. This, and I repeat once again, is very important.

Don't make the mistake of getting wrapped up in what everyone else is doing in that last week. Don't feel you have to go out and swim the entire course on Friday before the Sunday race because someone else is.

Go in with your pre-race plan and stick with it regardless of what is happening around you. YOU and YOU alone are the master of your destiny.

(39) CAREFUL WHAT YOU EAT!

Over my years of Ironman racing I've come to realize that not paying attention to detail can have a negative impact on how your race turns out.

Diet is no exception. There are lots of mistakes you can make in the final week, and during the race, that can lead to disaster.

Personally, I could never understand how people could train hard all year, stay with a proper training diet for months and then come to the race and eat restaurant food every day. Especially in the final 2 or 3 days leading up to the race.

I'm all for supporting the restaurant industry of the host city, but usually restrict visiting restaurants to 5 or 6 days before the race and of course anytime after. If you have no other option, be careful with your choices. You can't go too wrong with salads and most pastas, but try and avoid anything too exotic. If you have any allergies, be extra careful what you consume.

Every race I've ever done, including Hawaii, I made sure I had a motel with a kitchenette. My first day there I would go shopping and cook all my own meals. I would not stray from the diet I'd been on for the past 6 months.

I just can't put into words how important your food choices are in that last week. It's absolutely vital that when the gun goes off for the swim start, you do not have a queasy stomach. That can easily happen if you mess up your diet in the last few days.

Know exactly what your menu plan is before you even leave home. Plan your pre- race meals well before you even arrive in town. Also know what time you plan to eat those meals. As I mentioned earlier, I always finished my last meal on race eve by 4 p.m. I always finished my race morning breakfast 3 hours before the race start. This worked perfectly for me and I never had any sort of digestive problems when I stuck with this program.

Also, be careful at the carbo pre-race dinner. Choose your food carefully. In the later years of my career, I just stuck with salads and rolls and bottled drinks or else I didn't go to the dinner at all.

Early in my career I had the misfortune of not paying attention and having pasta with a different looking sauce at a pre-race dinner. I didn't realize that it was a clam sauce and I am allergic to shellfish. Needless to say, I became very ill and my race was ruined after training for an entire year.

So in case you feel I'm being a bit paranoid, I learned my lesson early and believe me, it never happened again. Don't let it happen to you.

That final week, be aware of what you're consuming.

That also applies to the race course itself. When you get to those aid stations (especially on the run) you will find cookies, oranges, power bars, power gels, grapes, chicken soup, and any number of things depending on the location of the race.

When you start running out of energy and feel you just can't go on, the natural instinct is to try everything at the aid stations in search of the right combination that will make you feel better and give you some much needed energy. This is a recipe for disaster. usually the opposite happens and you just end up feeling ill, and in the worst possible scenario, can't keep going and drop out.

My suggestion is to stick as close as possible to what you trained with. Go with what got you there. If you took power bars and gels on your bike and run training days, then stick with them during the race.

It's a misconception anyway that you have to keep eating all the way through the entire race. I believe the most important time to eat is at the start of the bike leg with the idea of keeping a steady balance of fuel for the entire 112 miles. That would mean taking on solid nutrition of some sort every hour or so.

If you've done that, eating during the marathon isn't really that important.

In my best ever Ironman marathon, I kept a steady pace without walking for the entire 26 miles and never ate a thing. All I took was 5-6 ounces of water at every aid station. That was it. I never remember feeling better out on the run course.

Ultimately, thinking through your diet leading up to the race can prevent any last minute problems, and ensure you feel great when that gun goes off and throughout the rest of the day.

(40) AVOID THE HYPE

If you're heading for your first Ironman you will find there are a lot of things going on when you get to the venue.

It's easy to get carried away, but it's important that you don't get too caught up in all the pre-race hype.

The merchandise tent will open and will be full of t-shirts, jackets, sweaters and almost anything you can think of that will have that particular Ironman name and year on it.

It's always nice to buy some of these items, but I would suggest waiting until after the race before you make your really big purchases.

It's after the race that the merchandise marked "finisher" will appear. That's what you want to be sure and get your hands on. It can be expensive, so allow for it in your budget. Some people tend to go overboard before the race and stock up on merchandise. They don't seem to realize that when they finish the race, the official finisher merchandise will have a lot of meaning to them.

Keep in mind that "Ironman" is a trademark and this merchandise is available at race sites only.

Usually on Wednesday the Expo tents will open. This is where you really have to be careful not to get carried away. You will see dozens of products including nutritional supplements, footwear, swim goggles, wetsuits, bike equipment, bikes etc. Most will proclaim to make your Ironman easier or faster.

It may be true or not, but it's a huge mistake to try new things in a race that is only 3 or 4 days away. This is not the time to be making equipment changes that you have not tested for weeks or months at home.

Even more serious is introducing a new drink or new food (energy) supplement to your race when you have not had the opportunity to try it in training.

My suggestion is, if you really like something you see and would like to try it, do it this way.

Buy it to try when you return home and begin training again. Most suppliers will have website addresses where you can also purchase their items at a later date. However, prices are sometimes better at race venues because there are no shipping costs incurred.

I'm not saying the products are not good, I'm just saying that most will take some getting used to. You have to be sure that it works for you. An Ironman race day is not the place to experiment.

Don't get caught up in the hype.

(41) RACE EVE

Oh my God!!

One day to go until my first Ironman!

What on earth do I do on that last day?

If you are preparing for your first race, you will soon be facing this question.

Here are a few things to do and not to do on that last day.

Whatever you do, don't do a hard workout of any sort.

As I mentioned earlier, remember to do a short workout (around 20 minutes) in each event. If your bike is checked in, then the swim and run is fine as well. Mark Allen suggests 10 X 10 second sprints in each discipline the day before a race. I've tried his method and it works quite well. Those short bursts of energy have a way of easing the pre-race tension. Whatever method you choose, just be sure to keep it short.

Do not go down to the expo and spend hours on your feet wandering around.

Visit the expo earlier in the week, not on the eve of the race. Stay away from crowds if at all possible.

Don't eat anything strange, and if possible, stay out of restaurants on that final day. Hopefully you will have a kitchenette and can make your own meals. If not, use caution when making your food choices.

I repeat once again. Don't eat too late on your last evening. Personally, I found that eating my last large meal no later than 4 p.m. on the eve of the race worked the best for me.

I will repeat this as well because it's important. Stay out of the direct sunlight!

If there is any check-in business to take care of, do it as early in the day as possible.

If there is a compulsory pre-race meeting on the eve of the race, be sure to go, but when it's over, leave. Go back to your room and read this book. Be sure to read "the Ironman on a glass of water," "what's your fear factor" and over and over again, "the Ironman bubble."

I ran into Dave Scott after one compulsory pre-race meeting on the eve of a race. I had a conversation with him about what to do on that last day.

He said most people are so nervous they go to the pre-race meeting, they go the expo, they wander around in the sun getting themselves tired and dehydrated and even more nervous.

His advice to me was this:

"Do what you have to do. Then get away from the crowds. Get out of the sun. Get away from all that nervous energy and pre-race jitters. Go to your room, put your feet up. Rest and relax. Eat early, be sure you're properly hydrated."

He was 100% right. I did that and I did it every race after that. It was exactly the correct thing to do.

I hope this advice helps you make it through that final day. Just remember the training is done. This is what it has been all about and soon you will be rewarded.

(42) AND SO IT BEGINS

I remember my first Ironman race day right down to the smallest detail. Years from now yours will be permanently engraved in your memory as well.

I asked myself many times over the course of the training year what on earth I was doing. How could I expect to do this race? Often there was an overwhelming feeling of being in way over my head.

For the first time I began to truly understand the term "looking into the eye of the tiger". Many times my instinct was to turn and run from this tiger called 'Ironman'. It can be an awe inspiring and fearsome challenge when you face it head on.

I will be eternally grateful that somehow I found the inner strength to push aside my fears and stare the tiger down.

So many individuals are capable of so much, but never test their limits -- never really find out how amazing they really are.

If you have made it this far -- to Ironman race day -- you have already learned much about yourself. Believe me, you are about to learn a lot more before the day is over.

As you wander the transition area, numbers on your arms and legs, fussing over your bike, taking care of last minute details, reflect on how far you have come since the day you were "Ironstruck".

Just for having made it to this moment you have my heartfelt admiration, because I know exactly what you're feeling. I know the inner turmoil you have mastered to get to this day.

You are my hero.

Now, if you listen, they are calling you to the start line. Your great adventure is about to begin...

(43) A GLASS OF WATER

If I could take one thing back from all the Ironman training I did over the years, it would be the thousands of laps I did in the pool with the hopes of thrashing out a faster swim time.

If you are an age grouper or a novice Ironman, there is really no point in spending hours and hours in the pool if you are already at the point where you can easily handle the distance. To devote your valuable training time to enable you to complete the swim 4 or 5 minutes faster is a very poor return on your time investment.

It seems that there are many Ironman athletes out there who push way too hard in the swim. The excess energy you burn in that opening leg is simply not recoverable and won't be there for the bike and run.

I firmly believe the reason so many people hit the wall in the marathon, is because they expended so much in the swim. The bike leg just finishes the job of depleting your resources.

There's no medal for swimming fast. There's not even a t-shirt if you swim fast and don't cross the finish line. Even being the very first out of the water means little if you can't put the three events together.

Take for example Kona, 1984. The winning swimmer was Djan Madruga. You might be asking yourself, "who the heck is he?" My point exactly. Djan was a world class swimmer and he beat the likes of Dave Scott, Mark Tinley and Mark Allen out of the water that day. However, Djan ran a 4:47 marathon and Dave Scott ran a 2:53.

This is where my theory comes in of running an Ironman like your energy, strength and endurance are all contained in a full glass of water when the start gun sounds.

Try and avoid expending half of that glass of water before you even get on the bike. That means your glass could well be down to the last quarter, or less, before you even put on your running shoes. I really believe there is a direct relationship between the Ironman shuffle and a poorly executed swim.

I remember the race where I finally began to understand pace and how best to nurse that all important glass of water right up to the last mile of the marathon.

It began with learning how to swim easier and more efficiently, and not faster. I learned how to relax in the water and to use looooonnnng, smoooooth, strokes. I couldn't believe how good I felt in the swim/bike transition. I probably used less than a quarter of that glass of energy.

For the first 40 km. of the bike I let myself get into the rhythm of the change of demands on my body before I settled into the race pace I felt I could hold for the remaining 140 km.

I could *not* believe the run. Normally, it was a struggle from mile one. This time I seemed to settle into a rhythm that I could maintain from the very beginning and the usual tiny voice telling me to walk because it hurt so much, never appeared.

To emphasise my point, I remember beginning to count the athletes I passed as the marathon progressed. It was a way of keeping my mind occupied and when I reached 350 that I had passed, I just quit counting, because it became a chore, there were so many.

Needless to say, everyone I passed was either faster than me in the swim, on the bike, in transition or possibly all three. The whole point is, it doesn't really matter how fast they were up to that point if they're walking now. Why spend hours and hours learning to swim faster if you're going to walk most of the marathon?

144

Just do the math. Say I'm running about an 8:15 pace like I did that year, from start to finish, and I pass someone at mile 10 and they have begun to walk and end up walking most of the marathon? They'll probably cross that finish line about 2 hours after me. That's the same person who swam faster and biked faster than I did. I had half a glass of water left and they were on empty at mile ten of the marathon.

I believe the best place to empty that glass is about 1 kilometer from the finish line. It's about there that the fan support has grown to huge proportions and, most important of all, you can hear the race announcer at the finish line. Those two happenings will carry you to the finish line. At that point, nothing is going to stop you.

I also think it's best to be on empty just before the finish, because like me, if you finish and feel great and have a fast recovery, you most likely crossed the finish line with a quarter of a glass left.

And hey! You don't want to wonder years down the road if you left something out on the course that day.

(44) DO YOU DOUBT YOURSELF?

The training is all behind you now.

Your attempt at Ironman immortality is at hand. All the demons are beginning to surface and self-doubt is leading the way. Followed closely by that inevitable question, "what on earth have I gotten myself into?"

Fear not. It's quite possible that pretty well every Ironman newbie has had exactly those same feelings as the big day arrives.

There seems to be a couple of reasons why almost everyone deals with this same issue. For one thing, you've put an immense amount of time and effort into your preparation. You've given up a lot and most likely family and social life have been put on hold.

The thought of failing and letting down everyone who has supported your preparation can become overwhelming if you dwell on it. Of course, the ultimate goal is to reach the elusive finish line, but keep in mind the long list of accomplishments you have achieved by reaching the start line.

Maybe you had to learn how to swim, or had never been anywhere near a triathlon bike, but now can ride for miles. Possibly you were a bit out of shape and not particularly pleased with what you saw when you looked in the mirror. Maybe your self-confidence was at a pretty low ebb. Let's face it, sometimes life can get a little stagnant and repetitive and it seems nothing will ever change it.

Then one day, something pretty amazing happened. You were "Ironstruck." Something moved you about this event and a spark was ignited that brought about a stunning metamorphosis.

Well, look at you now! You have certainly come a long, long way.

You are most likely in the best shape of your life. You have a better understanding of diet and nutrition, training and resting and of sacrifice and accomplishment.

You are already a new, improved version of yourself and as result have done something very special for those who care about you. All this, and you have yet to start the race. You simply cannot fail, because of what you have already accomplished, you have won.

So, don't fear the Ironman. Embrace it. Go to the waters edge with confidence. Feel the remarkable power, spirit and exhilaration that builds as anticipation makes way for action. Take comfort in the fact that you are not alone, and at that moment in time, you are an integral part of the fittest single group of people in the world.

Have confidence in your preparation. You have earned the right to participate. That spark that was ignited months ago has led you down this path.

Welcome the challenge and soon you will come to know what you are truly capable of. You will leave your comfort zone and surpass physical, mental and emotional limits that you would never have thought possible. Soon, that tiny spark that was kindled so long ago will become a glow that will stay with you forever.

(45) WHAT'S YOUR FEAR FACTOR?

What scares you the most about your upcoming Ironman race? What's your fear factor?

As fit as a person is going into their first Ironman, the fear factor is in the equation as the big day creeps ever closer.

As cool and confident as many participants may appear, there is almost always something that fills them with a certain amount of misgiving and anxiety.

For many, the fear can be overwhelming if it's not harnessed. It's almost like diving off a high cliff. Once you commit yourself, there is no turning back. After all, everyone in your circle of family, friends, and co-workers know all about it. For months they have observed as you have immersed yourself in your race preparation. How could you possibly back out and face the people who have supported you as you prepared for the race of your life?

Well, some people can and do back out. I recall one story in the early 80's that took place in the Hawaii Ironman.

The story went like this. At the conclusion of the swim portion of the race and all the swimmers were off the course, it was discovered that one person was missing. In other words, someone who was signed in for the swim had not arrived. Apparently they searched the entire course with scuba divers looking for the missing swimmer and feared the worst.

As it turns out, the missing swimmer had never entered the water. He decided he just could not do it and left the transition area and went for breakfast at a local restaurant. When he returned for his bike, he asked someone what all the fuss was about, and then, much to the relief of all concerned, the mystery was solved.

It seems that the swim is particularly terrifying for many who are attempting their first Ironman. I count myself in that group. People have been known to stand on the shore in tears, unable to face the swim even long after the gun has sounded. Some have been coaxed into the water by volunteers and ended up doing just fine. Normally, just a few hundred meters into the swim, nervousness will disappear and it becomes easier to settle into the race.

In my first Ironman in Hawaii, I will never forget the amazing euphoria in the transition tent after the swim. More than anything, I believe it was relief, because for many, myself included, a very big hurdle had been cleared. As far as I was concerned that day, there was nothing that would stop me from becoming an Ironman once I conquered the swim. There was no doubt, the water was my fear factor.

I believe that most who are considering their first Ironman are runners. Also, pretty well everyone has biked at one time or another in their life, but really few have had the opportunity or reason to swim in the open water. So it makes sense that a lot of novice ironmen will be extremely apprehensive about the swim.

Some I suppose, may fear the bike. Maybe steep hills or cycling in close proximity to so many others will cause some concern. However, in the bike or run you have complete control. You can just stop or slow down. I think it's fair to say, that in the swim, once one is half a mile out in the open water, you are pretty well committed.

Personally, I think much of the fear grows all out of proportion as the race nears. Keep in mind that race preparation is much more than swim, bike, run. You must also prepare yourself mentally.

When the fear of failure begins to haunt you, it's time to take a step back and consider how far you have come.

It may not seem like it on race day, as you are surrounded by hundreds of athletes, but in the big scheme of things, few people in the world will ever attempt what you are about to do. Believe in your training, your preparation and ability. When the fear seems overwhelming as the race nears, regardless if it's the swim or the bike or just fear of failing, remember this:

There are hundreds of other athletes who will feel the same as you on race morning. That is one of the things that makes this event so amazing. You are all on the same journey together. The goal is a common one. Take comfort in this united spirit as it will help take you through the day.

There will be several thousand volunteers and thousands more spectators and friends and relatives who will all play a part in your quest for that distant finish line.

They will be behind you when your fear is greatest, your inspiration when you doubt and your strength when you tire.

You are truly amazing just to reach the start line of an Ironman Triathlon. Just to have gotten to that point makes you a resounding success, so how can you possibly fail?

You may have felt at one time that you would never reach this moment, yet here you are. Fit and proud along with 2000 others on race morning awaiting the starting gun. You are in the best condition of your life and have the admiration of everyone around you as you embark on this great adventure.

If you are about to attempt your first Ironman, may the Iron Gods of Kona, who haunt the searing lava fields of the King K. highway, smile upon you and very soon welcome you into the most amazing family on earth.

(46) BE SURE TO PACK LIGHT

One Ironman race morning I watched in awe as an industrious triathlete attempted to tape a full size foot pump to his bike. Air cartridges were available at the time and I estimate his pump weighed about the same as 150 of those.

I never stayed around to see how that episode ended, but hopefully he didn't get it to fit and went to plan B. Whatever that was.

During another race, on the bike course, I passed a rider who had a pack the size of a small country on his back. It sort of made the aerodynamic brake pads on his $6000 bike a waste of technology. All I could think was that he was planning a picnic along the way and was packing a blanket, a bottle of wine and food for two.

For most, the goal is to just finish the race and in that case it's not necessary to worry about every ounce of weight. However, it is counter productive to go overboard. Too much weight will cause you to expend energy you can't afford to lose. Normally, I would take four water bottles. One for water and three for my replacement drink. My drink of choice isn't available at Ironman aid stations. I would leave another three bottles at special needs. I picked up a fresh water bottle at every aid station. If you are happy with what the aid stations are providing, then you can go super light and just take one bottle for water and one for Gatorade or whatever else the stations are supplying and replace them both at every station.

Also, be inventive when it comes to carrying food on your bike. Try and put it where it is least likely to get in the way or cause a lot of drag. Gels are a great choice because they are light, easily taped to the frame and take up little room.

Two spare tires should be sufficient or in case of "really" bad luck, you can take a small patch kit as well. Air cartridges are a great choice and will fit into a small pouch along with your two spares and a tire lever. This small pouch will fit behind or under your seat.

Be aware of your clothing as well. Especially in races like Penticton where it is often cool in the early morning as you exit the swim, and hot for most of the late morning and afternoon. Overdress and you will pay for it later as it heats up. Too many clothes will cause you to overheat and you will soon have to get rid of long sleeve shirts and jackets somewhere. Keep in mind that you most likely will never see them again. A tri-suit or swimsuit for women or swimsuit with top for men are better options, with arm warmers to ward off the early morning cold. Don't use your expensive arm warmers. Use a pair of long sports socks with the toes cut off and just discard them at an aid station when no longer needed. Leave an old sweater in special needs in case the weather turns nasty. Again, remember, you won't see your special needs items after the race. Clothes are normally given to charity.

If ever you want to travel light, it's in the run. Every single spare ounce will weigh a proverbial ton over the course of the marathon. Water bottles will drive you to distraction. As mentioned in "run equipment" an Ironman fuel belt is a great choice. The distribution of weight makes so much more sense than a single water bottle. Three or four gels in the back of a jersey will feel like they are wearing a hole in your back if they keep banging against you every step you take. A single energy bar will soon increase from 10 ounces to 10 pounds. Mark my words. You will find enough bars, clothes and water bottles along the marathon course to open your own store. It's all because of the weight.

Have a plan in place before the big day arrives and think light to ensure as much comfort as possible on race day.

(47) THE IRONMAN BUBBLE

I was recently asked, "what does an Ironman think about during the race?"

Good question.

It's a good question because there is just so much happening during an Ironman. There is chaos all around you and a hundred distractions. By its very nature the race is as much a mental and emotional battle as it is a physical one.

I truly believe that the majority of novice ironmen train their hearts out, yet fail to realize the importance of how to approach the race with a plan in mind long before the starting gun sounds. What makes the Ironman such a special event and such an amazing accomplishment, is the ability it has to test and challenge every aspect of a persons capabilities. The Ironman is about so much more than having a perfectly toned body, the best equipment, or the ideal diet.

When you look into the eye of the tiger on race morning, it is essential that you are prepared to push all fears and doubts aside and devote your energy to the task at hand.

The term "in the zone" might sound familiar.

'The state where you block out all the distractions that could keep you from reaching your ultimate goal. Doubts and fears take a backseat to confidence, understanding, potential, and the possibility that something magical can happen beyond what you ever thought possible."

Mark Allen calls it the State of Discovery.

"In Shamanism, it is referred to as the space between two thoughts where your intuition takes over. It's a quiet alertness where answers come and life is created in just about any way you can imagine it. It is total absorption in making the unimaginable and impossible happen. It is the ability to let fears fall by the wayside because no room exists for them in your focus and attention. In short, you are too busy functioning at your highest level to waste energy on being fearful or contemplating failure."

This in my mind, is the very essence of the Ironman and why achieving your Ironman goals is such a life altering event. Read that last line once again.

You are too busy functioning at your highest level to waste energy on being fearful or contemplating failure.

What an accomplishment if you can make this a reality in every aspect of your life! Well, it's exactly what happens over and over again to those who are "Ironstruck" and are driven to take up the Ironman challenge. They develop a new and better understanding of what they are truly capable of and see the world in a far different light.

To simplify it, I like to call it the "Ironman bubble."

From the moment the start gun sounds, imagine yourself in your own protective bubble. Have a swim plan in mind and stay on the edge of the mass of swimmers. Stay detached from the chaos happening nearby. Forget about fears and doubts. Focus on the task at hand. Let nothing stop you from reaching your ultimate goal. If someone does happens to crash into you, let them bounce off and carry on like it never happened. resume your calm, relaxed stroke. Stay in your own space.

As the race wears on, even more things begin to happen and distractions are everywhere.

The marathon is the ultimate test of your concentration and determination.

Almost anything can and will happen all around you. Spectators yelling, frenetic aid stations. Ambulances screaming up and down the highway. People walking. Being sick. Passing out. Relieving themselves on the side of the road. Energy bars, water bottles, and clothing litter the highway. Items that once weighed little, now weigh a ton. You have blisters. You are hot. Every muscle in your body hurts. Every part of who you are is being put to the test. Every fibre screams at you to stop NOW, but ...

You are in your bubble. The chaos is outside the bubble and you want to be in that zone where no outside distraction will keep you from reaching your ultimate goal. You have no energy to waste on negative thoughts or fear of failure. All your focus is on the finish line now as it gets ever closer.

I can't stress enough how important it is to prepare for the mental and emotional aspects of the Ironman.

In the months before the race (especially in the last few weeks) visualize yourself in that zone, in that bubble. It's your space. Commit yourself to focusing on the ultimate goal with no fear and doubts standing in your way.

I believe you will be amazed when you discover what you are truly capable of.

(48) THE SWIM

Your first Ironman swim. You've come so far and now the big day is here. The beach is so crowded. You look around with apprehension, and possibly just plain fear. Your heart is racing and you wonder if you even belong here.

Of course you do. You've worked long and hard for this. What you need is a solid plan for the swim and then you can enjoy it.

Ask 100 triathletes which of the three events is most important in determining your final result and this is what you will most likely hear.

-- about 80% will say the marathon. The reasoning is that if you a really poor day on the Ironman marathon course it will determine if and how you finish the race.

-- around 18% will say the bike leg because it is the longest in distance.

-- the other 2% will say it is the swim. I am in that 2%.

The energy you can use up through inefficient swimming and fighting your way through the pack is lost for the day. You will not get it back for the bike and the run. It's almost impossible to calculate how important a stress free, efficient swim will be to your final result.

After much trial and error, I've come to the realization that the swim is the most important leg of the Ironman. It goes a long way toward deciding the outcome of the next two events.

Most novice ironmen have similar swim plans. Usually navigating in the open water is an issue for them so they decide they will just follow the buoys (swim markers) all the way to the big marker indicating the turn. Or else they plan to wait for 50 or 60 seconds and then follow the markers.

Trust me when I say, this is the biggest mistake you can make and it will make your swim miserable and will dictate how the rest of your day goes. If you are fast enough to get out with the leaders then start where you want. That means you can do the course in around 55 minutes. That will not be most of you.

I tried the lane marker thing and believe me, it is NOT the way to go. Waiting for a minute doesn't help much either. Look around you and you will see hundreds of other first timers waiting with you. Either way you will be kicked, punched, shoved under water, swam over and nearly drowned. And that's in just the first 10 minutes. It can go on for a long time. It's no way to start your first Ironman race.

Several years ago I was looking at an overhead picture of an Ironman swim start and it suddenly dawned on me where I should have been swimming all those years.

My next race I tried my theory out and I could not believe how much I enjoyed the swim. I felt relaxed the whole time. I never got kicked or punched or run into once and I came out of the water feeling like I'd hardly worked. AND, I had a personal best time by 5 minutes.

Now I'll tell you how to have a pressure free, relaxed Ironman swim.

First, make sure you have worked on your swim stroke to make it smooth, efficient and relaxed. It's a needless waste of energy to thrash your arms and legs as fast as you can for 2.4 miles.

Before the swim start make sure you are on the far outside of all the other swimmers. As far as you can go. You want to be the last person out there.

You don't want anyone on your outside. Well, maybe a few people, but not dozens. The marker buoys should be way over on your inside.
So to clarify, If the course is clockwise, the course markers and the bulk of the field will be on your right. If the course is counter clockwise the markers will be on your left.

When the gun signals the start of the race, wait 10 or 15 seconds (that's all) and pick your outside line, keeping everyone to your inside.

Start relaxed and smooth. Keep your heart rate down as much as possible.

The beauty of this system is that you hardly ever have to look up and try and find the big turn marker. The entire field will eventually collapse toward the lane markers as the turn nears. You just collapse right along with them, always staying on the outside. When you are coming up on the marker, try not to swim right towards it. This is the natural tendency, but will result in more traffic problems. I used to even try and bump against it when I turned and then I would get clobbered by everyone else doing the same thing.

Make your turn 5 or 6 meters away from it if you have to. It will get just as deadly around that marker as it was at the start. Everyone seems to gravitate toward it, feeling this is a good way to save time.

The few extra seconds you take to swim wide around the marker will be paid back many times over. If you get in that crush at the beginning or at the turns, you lose TONS of time and also increase your heart rate from the anxiety. Not only that, it interrupts the smoothness of your stroke and your rhythm. It makes you waste energy that you will need later in the day.

Use this system for the entire swim. It doesn't matter if it's out and back or out and back twice. You'll find that as you get further into the race, the swimmers will be more spread out and you will probably be closer to the markers. That's o.k., as long as nobody is on your outside. By making sure your outside is free of traffic as possible, you eliminate the chances of someone running into you. Or at the very least you minimize it.

Use this system and trust me that it works, and I guarantee it will take a lot of the worry and stress away from your first Ironman swim.

You will feel great when you get out of the water and excited about getting on your bike.

(49) THE SWIM TO BIKE TRANSITION

This is the best way to approach the swim to bike transition.

The first thing that will happen when you stand up after your swim is that you will have a moment of dizziness. It is brief and normal. Don't forget you have basically been laying flat throughout the swim and need a few seconds to regain your equilibrium.

First thing to remember.

Do not run because others are!

This is not a good strategy and serves no good purpose. If you followed my swim advice, then you have come out of the water feeling very good about your swim split. Maybe you were even pleasantly surprised when you became aware of your finish time.

More importantly, you are relaxed and your heart rate is not all out of control. Your breathing is even. That is perfect! Keep it like that throughout the transition. Don't get excited and try and rush. You are here to finish this race. At this point, rushing to save 15 seconds will hurt more than it helps.

As soon as you stand up and have your balance, remove your cap and goggles. Follow the others towards the wetsuit strip area. As you walk, reach around and undo the small Velcro pad covering your zipper, grab the cord and pull the zipper all the way down the back of your wetsuit as far as it will go.

Pull the wetsuit off your arms and pull it as far down to your waist as you can. When you approach the two wetsuit strippers, lay down (on the grass I hope) and they will each grab one arm of your wetsuit and pull it off. when you stand up, they will hand it to you.

While carrying your swim gear, go to the bike gear racks and you will be given your first transition bag. If it's busy, get it yourself. You should always know exactly where your gear is located before the swim. I always count the rows beforehand.

In the transition tent, dump out your bike gear bag and put your swim gear in that bag. A volunteer may help you depending how busy it is. Don't worry about your bag with your swim gear getting lost. Just leave it right there. It will magically appear along with everything else after the race.

I found that the best system is to have all your equipment in that bag. Including helmet and shoes. I used to leave my shoes with the bike and most times they were not where I left them because the bikes are very close together and things get kicked around. It may be awkward to wear shoes from the tent to your bike, but that is part of my plan for you. It will make you walk and take your time because running in bike shoes is near impossible.

Remember. You don't want your heart racing. Stay relaxed and calm, regardless of what is going on all around you. Just like in the swim, ignore what everyone else is doing. Do not let anyone or anything dictate how you manage your race.

Walk at a good pace to your bike. This is just to stretch your legs out.

Don't grab one of those drinks on the way out. Don't eat anything.

You will have more fluid loss than you would think possible during the swim. It fools many people, because they're surrounded by water and can't seem to imagine it.

Regardless, don't eat or drink yet. Give your system about 15 minutes to adjust. Make sure your helmet is on properly. Next, *walk* your bike to the bike mounting area. Find a bit of an open spot off to the side if you can. This area of the transition can get quite congested. Some people are rushing and accidents happen here.

When you straddle your bike, click in one pedal. Then push off, and click the other in when you start moving. Don't make the mistake of pushing off without at least one foot locked into the pedals. Sometimes you just can't get them clicked in and maintain your balance at the same time. Bad things can happen. Always have one done before you start moving! Then if necessary, you can still pedal out of transition with one shoe clicked in and one out if necessary. Once you start moving, you have to keep moving. There will be bikes everywhere.

Make a note of this. Always leave your bike in a very easy gear before the race even starts. This is your "leaving transition gear."

I repeat! Stay alert! Accidents happen here!

Congratulations! You have completed the swim to bike transition.

(50) THE BIKE

As you spin away from transition in a nice easy, relaxing gear, watch out for other cyclists who will come flying by like they're in the last 500 meters of the bike course. Stay over to the right. You may just pass some of them later.

Ease yourself into the bike portion of the race. Give yourself about 15 minutes and then take a good drink to replace fluid lost during the swim. Make this drink your fluid replacement drink (sports drink) as opposed to water. Eat something 10 or 15 minutes after your drink. A power gel will do nicely.

Before the race you should set the timer on your watch to beep every 30 minutes. This works very well to keep you properly hydrated. Drink every 30 minutes and eat every 60 minutes. Start your timer after your first drink. Having a system set up before the race takes all the guesswork out of when you will eat and drink on the bike course.

Things to remember.

Never pass on the right. It's very dangerous!

Never draft. The Iron cops on motorcycles will definitely penalize you (a time penalty of normally five minutes) and you just may need those extra minutes at the end of the day.

Watch out for water bottles on the road. Sometimes they will fall out of someone's cage or they will drop one by accident. Hitting one of those the wrong way can end your day!

Stay away from the center line. It's dangerous out there and the Iron cops could get you for a center line infraction. They are trying to make the bike course safe. Always stay well right unless you are passing.

Whenever you encounter significant headwind make full use of your aero bars. This is not just so you can finish faster. It's so you can save your energy. By going into the aero position in a headwind you can travel 2-4 kph faster without working any harder! That is exactly what you want. Everything you do on race day should be centered around saving as much energy as possible. Your goal is to finish the 112 mile bike as economically as you can.

Concerning the steep up hills, a question commonly heard is, "should I sit or stand on the up hills?" My answer is to do both. Alternating standing and sitting gives you the opportunity to stretch out your legs. As a matter of fact, in my later Ironman races I would stand every 30 minutes or so (even on the flats). All you need is 25 or 30 seconds of standing to keep your legs from tightening up too much. It will pay dividends when you start your run. I used to do it in training all the time to make it more natural come race day.

If you are really new to cycling, some down hills can be very scary. Ironman Canada for instance has a huge fast downhill at Yellow Lake. You can easily hit speeds of 80 kph. It's just a great opportunity to get free kilometers. If at all possible go into the aero position for the whole downhill ride. Don't forget, highways like that are built for cars to handle 80 kph easily. It is safe. Just relax on your bike, stay to the right and let it go. If it's too scary for you, simply sit up. This will scrub off some speed and you will feel more in control. Try and avoid using your brakes if you can. You work hard on the up hills, and deserve the fast, free downhill kilometers when the opportunity arises. Be aware, however, of courses like Coeur d'Alene that have plenty of fast, sweeping downhill curves. Just watch for caution signs. If there's a sign, use your brakes.

When you reach the final 10 kilometers of the bike course, it's time to start thinking about the upcoming marathon. Do whatever you can to work out some of the stiffness in your arms and legs. Try and get the tenseness out of your shoulders. Do shoulder shrugs over and over as you bike toward transition. Stand up on your pedals and stretch out your legs. First one, then the other. Try and loosen your neck muscles. You want to be able to stay as relaxed as possible in the marathon.

Now as you approach transition, slow down. As you coast in toward the bike catchers, snap your shoes out of the pedals. Rest them lightly on top of the pedals so you can just hop (well, stagger) off the bike once they catch you. Leave your helmet done up until you are off the bike. Once you dismount, remove it and take it to the transiton tent with you.

Congratulations! You finished the Ironman bike!

(51) THE BIKE TO RUN TRANSITION

I know exactly what you'll be feeling when you get off that bike and enter the bike to run transition. First of all, you'll want to throw your bike in the lake. Secondly, the chance of somehow finishing the marathon distance the way your legs feel right at that moment seems pretty well impossible.

As you walk (hobble) into the transition tent, your heart may be sinking and you may feel you just cannot do it.

Believe me. You are not alone. This is a very common reaction.

And yes! You can do it! Remember, this is the last time you will leave the transition area. The next time you return, you will be home!

This is the moment where your resolve will be truly tested.

Keep in mind that if you have made it to this point, you have an excellent chance of finishing the race. There is plenty of time if you follow the suggestions I gave you in the run tips section.

Also, remember the energy you saved by having a calm, relaxed, energy saving swim. Believe it or not, you may well be in a lot better position than a lot of other people out on the run course.

Change into whatever you plan on wearing.

If you feel you need medical attention for anything, this is the time to do it. The medical tent is right there beside the transition tent.

A word of warning however. Don't stall. Get out there! You do have a time limit and spending 30-40 minutes in transition can lead to disappointment at the end of the day.

Gather yourself. Have a good drink and something to eat (a power gel would be good) before you head out on the run course.

And remember these immortal words.

"TRY NOT. DO. OR DO NOT. THERE IS NO TRY."

Yoda: The Empire Strikes back.

So get out there and DO it.

From now on, every single step you take brings you closer to the finish line and Ironman immortality.

(52) THE RUN

As you start out on the marathon course you will most likely experience several different emotions.

I used to find it very difficult at times to convince myself to leave the transition area. After a long hard bike it often feels that finishing the marathon distance would be next to impossible. It is at this point in the race that your determination and resolve may truly be tested. This is where the term "Ironman" begins to have meaning.

Remember that you are not alone in feeling this. There are hundreds of novice ironmen dealing with the same emotions. Keep in mind that you had an intelligent swim and conserved energy for this point in the race.

One thing I learned over the years is how much our bodies can withstand and just how much we are capable of if we dare to try. Often our spirit is conquered long before our physical energy is used up.

A good example is my last Ironman. At almost exactly the halfway point in the bike I had a bad crash. I lost focus for just a few seconds and slipped off the shoulder of the road. When I tried to recover the bike went over and I hit the road very hard. The last half of the bike was fairly difficult. As I sat in the transition tent my shoulder was extremely sore and it was only by experience that I knew my body could withstand quite a lot if I gave it a chance.

I was at the stage in my career where I felt this Ironman could well be my last and I did not want to end my career by dropping out of the race.

The marathon took me 5 hours and 5 minutes. The Ironman took me 14 hours and 15 minutes. I found out later that I had a separated shoulder. I sort of had a feeling that was the case but then I reasoned that I wasn't running on my hands, so things would work out.

I'm telling you this story because when you get to this point in the race you have to realize that no matter how sore and tired you feel, the ability your body has to recover will amaze you if you give it a chance.

As soon as you cross that run start mat, do your best to run. At first your stride will be very short and unnatural, but as your legs adjust to the demands of running you will begin to feel and run better. Run for as long as you can without stopping. You want to get some kilometers behind you. When and if you just 'have' to walk try and walk the aid stations and run in between as much as you can. When you do walk, try and walk at a fast pace.

Hopefully you practiced this in your training as I suggested in the run training suggestions. It makes a huge difference if you go into the Ironman with a race plan.

Be very careful at the aid stations when it comes to choosing your food and drink. The urge is to try some of everything as you try and find something to boost your energy. Many athletes have gotten sick during the marathon from making this mistake.

Really try not to mix your food and drink choices. I would suggest avoiding Coke and Pepsi until the last 6 or 7 miles. Remember that if you do start drinking it, then you should drink it at *every* aid station to follow or else you risk really upsetting your sugar balance.

One year I drank nothing but water at every station and did not eat at all. I felt good and didn't want to mess with it. I had my fastest ever Ironman marathon. So I think that goes to show it's not necessary to fill your body with grapes, bananas, cookies, and whatever else you have to choose from Just go with what worked for you all those months of training. If you trained with power gels, then race with power gels.

Try and make a point of not walking the down hills. I have seen many people do this and I could never understand it. You should take advantage of gravity every chance you get. Just like on the bike. If you plan on walking the up hills then be sure to run the down hills. Do everything you can to get those kilometers behind you without using up too much energy too soon.

Take heart in the fact that there are hundreds of you out there sharing the same dream. To finish the race. It is truly a beautiful thing when you see so many, so determined to reach a common goal.

Be careful should you decide to run with someone along the way. They may deviate quite a bit from what you have been doing and throw off your race plan. Sometimes it's best to run on your own. Read the "Ironman bubble" again.

It's always an uplifting moment when you make the final outward leg and turn for home for the last time. Now each kilometer that passes you feel a lift in your spirit.

In the final 6 or 7 kilometers you will most likely discover that you have an amazing amount of energy left. This happens over and over in the Ironman. For some reason, some sort of physical change takes place and many people have a sustained burst of energy.

You will also be lifted by an increasing number of spectators as you get nearer and nearer to the finish. Soon dozens turn to hundreds and you hear that amazing, welcome sound of the finish line announcer. This is when it will hit home that you are really going to do it! You are going to be an IRONMAN!

Be sure to take it all in, because this moment will be etched in your memory forever. No matter how many Ironman races you do, this is one you will never forget.

(53) WELCOME HOME

Your first Ironman finish and there is no way to truly describe the emotions you will feel as you complete the final few hundred meters. The Ironman is so much more than a race. It is an awakening of the spirit deep inside all of us. For many, their first Ironman and the months leading up to it have been a journey of self-discovery.

It is not easy to reach this point. The road to the finish line is strewn with broken dreams. In any given race six to twelve percent of those who start will not finish. So in fact, in just ten races somewhere around two thousand starters will not finish.

There is nowhere to hide in the Ironman. That is what makes it so great. It is you facing your demons alone. It is you who must look into the eye of the tiger and stare it down. The race by its very nature will challenge you in every possible way. That is what makes reaching the finish line a truly amazing accomplishment and one that will change you forever.

Being an Ironman looks good on any resumé. It shows dedication, focus, determination, strength of spirit, and courage. Believe me, when you succeed, you will become a member of something special. I'm sure the 'Iron Gods' of Kona smile each time a new addition is welcomed into the family. In the beginning of your journey you heard their challenge and now, indeed, you have shown them what you are made of.

I will leave you with this: Five years after I finished my first Ironman I received a Christmas card just out of the blue, postmarked Kona. It was from the Hawaii Ironman organizing committee. It only ever came that one year and I will cherish it forever. It had just two words on it besides Merry Xmas.

Two words that I hope can one day can be said to you.

ALOHA IRONMAN!

(54) SOMEBODY CATCH ME

As you cross the finish line, several things will happen. Firstly and most importantly, you can finally stop running. What happens next depends on the condition you are in when you reach the finish line.

This can vary from being on a tremendous high and feeling great or on the other end of the scale, being taken immediately to the medical tent.

Whatever the case, there is always someone there to help each and every triathlete as they arrive. They are the "catchers". This person will help you through the routine of the finishing area.

First of all they will take you to your finisher's t-shirt and medal. Guard these with your life no matter how bad you feel.

If you really do not feel well, you will be taken to the medical tent for observation. You will most likely be given an I.V. if you are dehydrated. Depending on how you feel after the first I.V., you may be given a second one. I believe the Ironman record is six or seven I.V.'s. A doctor decides how many you need. All medical aid is covered by the insurance you purchase with your entry. Be kind to the doctors and nurses. Most of them are volunteering their time for you.

If you feel o.k. at the finish, your catcher will take you to the massage tent. You may have to sign in if it's quite busy. It all depends on your finish time and luck. Normally the wait is not too long and the massage is amazing and well worth the wait.

Most finish areas will have hot tubs. Personally, I have never used one, but that is a personal choice. For me, the 2.4 mile swim was normally enough water for one day.

There is plenty to eat and drink and I would highly recommend finding a replacement drink as soon as possible. Do this before you eat and when you do eat, take it real easy. Your system will be out of sync for a while.

When you feel like you'd like to leave the finish area, ask any volunteer where the transition bags are. All your bags from the day will be together. Trust me, this is not the easiest part of the day. You have lots of wet gear and different bags to deal with. This is where you will be glad if you listened to me and put an empty backpack in your dry strip bag. (The one you tossed on the pile that contains the clothes you wore race morning). Stuffing a few of your transition bags into the backpack will really make things more manageable for you. Hopefully you followed my advice as well concerning a bike pump. Don't take one race morning! There will be pumps there. You don't want to have to carry one around as you leave transition.

Don't forget! You have your bike to take out as well. The finish area is secure and nobody can come in to help you. However, if you can somehow arrange to have them meet you as you exit, they can help you with your gear.

It all depends on them seeing you arrive at the finish line and when you decide to leave transition. It can be a difficult thing to organize. Usually, you will be on your own for some time with all your gear.

Personally, I enjoyed the finish area experience. There are a lot of really happy people there. They may be sore, but at the same time, it will be slowly sinking in that they have accomplished something really special.

Take it all in and enjoy your time in the finish area even if you do feel a bit disorientated and weak. It's a really special time for you since you have just completed your first Ironman.

(55) THE MORNING AFTER

When you wake up the morning after finishing your first Ironman, you will be overwhelmed by several things. First of all it will hit you that you have just succeeded in one of the most difficult challenges of your life. You will also ache in almost every fibre of your body.

Despite the pain, you will be on top of the world. YOU are an Ironman. Believe me the pain becomes insignificant once you succeed in your quest for the finish line. As a matter of fact, in a way, you will welcome it as a testament to the effort it required to reach your goal.

Chances are, shortly after you crossed the finish line the day before, you swore to yourself you would never, never put yourself through this again. You will be "amazed" how quickly you will forget how much you hurt right at that moment. Almost overnight you will be wondering where the registration will be for the next years race.

As for getting out of bed the morning after, well, that is another story. You will most likely feel that you'll never walk the same again. Trust me, it gets better.

First of all, when you first get up, you would be wise to have some sort of replacement drink, because your body was asked to perform above and beyond during the race and must be refueled. As much as the thought of drinking anything might disgust you, it's a very important step to aid in a speedy recovery.

Have a nice long shower. You may have to do some serious scrubbing to get those magic marker numbers to disappear from your arms and legs. You may not *want* to make them disappear completely. It is not unusual to see faint race numbers all over town, worn proudly as a badge of honor, until days later when they slowly disappear on their own. Usually your ID bracelet will still be on when you get back home. Some Ironman finishers have been know to put on their finisher t-shirts the morning after and leave them on for a week.

This is important advice when it comes to your finisher's t-shirt. You will only ever get one. No matter how many of these amazing races you attempt, you will only ever get one "first" Ironman finisher shirt. Wear it for a week or so and then clean it well and store it away. This will be really important to you years down the road. Just looking at mine now -- over 20 years later -- brings back such a rush of amazing memories of that first time I crossed the finish of my first Ironman in Kona. Sometimes I wonder how many of these t-shirts still remain in my Canada. I remember, despite this being a big country, there were only around 50 Canadians in Hawaii in 1984. I could well have one of the few t-shirts left from that race.

Don't forget, once you are officially recorded as a finisher, you can purchase the Ironman Trademark finisher clothes that are on sale for that year. Make sure you bring along extra money for this. These are finisher clothes you can wear year round at home after you pack your finish line t-shirt away.

O.K. When you get out of the shower, it's time to eat something. Your digestive system may be in a bit of a mess, but don't worry, this soon goes away and you will be eating everything is sight later in the day. For breakfast however take it a bit easy.

After you have something to eat, "get out that door and go for a walk!" As brutal as that may sound, it's for the best. Plus you have to find a newspaper anyway. Don't leave it too long because souvenir newspapers *fly* off the rack the morning after the race. It has the entire race story and who knows, your picture might even be in it.

In later years, I started going for an easy run the morning after. Yes! A run! Just an easy walk at first. Then stretch it out into longer strides. Then try and run really, really easy for a minute or so. Do this a few times. You will be amazed how much this will speed up your recovery. In later years, I was able to run 15 or 20 minutes quite easily the day after.

Some prefer to go for a swim, but I always found that took too much work to go to the beach and change and dry off etc. A simple easy jog always worked the best.

I used to love taking that morning after paper and finding a really great coffee shop. I would read through the entire race story. Often you will run into lots of other ironmen who will be more than happy to share their race experience with you. It's just a really great day.

By early afternoon, (after entering for the next year, if I had decided to) I was ready to make the fast food run. Every Ironman town or city has a "fast-food" street. I would walk up and down that street and have all those forbidden foods I had passed up during training. Fried chicken, pizza, french fries, maybe a hamburger, and my all time favorite, ice cream. Treat yourself. You earned it.

If you go on to do even more of these incredible races, you will develop your own morning after ritual. You will find ways that you just love to spend that day. It soon becomes a part of your own personal Ironman tradition.

Regardless how you spend the next day, enjoy it! You have joined a very special group. You have become part of the Ironman family and that will be yours to cherish forever.

(56) NOW WHAT?

Tackling your first Ironman is a great springboard to a new and better way of life.

Use the opportunity it provides to adopt a lifestyle of health and fitness.

Perhaps when you first decided you wanted to cross that finish line, it became your all consuming goal and you never really thought much about what your objectives would be once you realized your dream.

It's such a perfect time to seize the opportunity and make a commitment to a better and more satisfying way of life that will pay you dividends for years to come.

Consider what you will have learned during the time spent preparing for your first Ironman attempt.

Most likely you will have learned quite a lot about practicing proper diet. Possibly you came to realize the value of vitamin supplements, proper hydration, and a variety of other training aids that you never really knew much about until you were bitten by the Ironman bug.

Now you may possibly know about the value of chiropractic treatments, massage therapy, visualization and heart monitors.

It would be wise to try and avoid focusing on that one day when you tackle your first Ironman. It can lead to the "what now?" question which in turn can result in bouts of depression that sometimes happen when a long sought after goal is realized.

Regardless of how the race itself turns out, consider that you are probably in the best physical condition of your life, thanks to your pursuit of the Ironman finish line.

Seize upon that and make a commitment to maintaining your healthy lifestyle for good. It doesn't mean you have to train like an Ironman for your entire life. It means eating right and staying fit regardless if you ever take part in another race or not.

Your physical well being is probably the best gift you can give to your family and others who care about you.

So consider making the finish line of the Ironman just the beginning of something very special and not your final destination.

(57) AVOIDING BURNOUT

For many, reaching the Ironman finish line just once is their main objective. Certainly it's a worthy goal, because it makes you a member of a very special family. More and more novice ironmen are taking up the challenge, but still, it is a very small segment of the world population that will ever have this experience.

However, there are some who return year after year to yet another race and it becomes a constant cycle of training, dieting, racing and sacrificing all else to relive the magic.

I know from experience, what a heavy toll this can take on your body and also the family, career and social aspects of your life. It's extremely important to consider how year after year of tackling the Ironman can impact your life and the life of those around you.

From a physical stand point, even if you are single and live on your own, it might be wise to consider giving yourself a bit of a mental and physical break from the rigors of Ironman preparation.

At one stretch, I raced in the Ironman for nine years in a row. It seemed that after reaching the finish line for the first time, each race after that presented a new set of challenges. To swim faster, run the marathon without stopping, achieve a personal best overall time, or even place in any age group. There are always new challenges in this event.

Like many, I believed that the more I raced and the more I trained, the more experience I would have and the faster I would go. That was true for a few years, but then I started to slide backwards. Regardless of how much I trained, or how long I prepared for a race, I just could not improve. My times began to get slower.

In hindsight, I believe it was physical burnout brought on by years and years of constant training with insufficient rest. In my last few races I reverted back to where I started. I just wanted to experience the atmosphere and finish the race any way I could. Unfortunately, there really is no halfway in the Ironman. Just to reach the finish line and meet all the time splits along the way requires quite a lot of preparation.

I really believe that if you are planning a long career, it's wise to take a complete year or two off after you've competed in 3 or 4 Ironman races. This will let your body fully recover and will also give you time to get back in touch with the other aspects of your life that were sort of put on the back burner while you pursued your goals.

It doesn't necessarily mean letting yourself fall completely out of shape. There's no reason that you can't stay fit and compete in shorter races. Run some ten K races, Olympic distance tri's or maybe plan one marathon a year. Go for nice relaxing swims and go for easy bike rides in the country. Don't worry about times and splits and training schedules. Stay physically active 3 or 4 days a week to maintain your fitness, but make it enjoyable and easy. At the same time maintain a good sound diet and get tons of rest.

When you resume Ironman training after giving yourself a long rest, you will be completely recovered and should have no problem settling back into your training program. You may even find that you have the race of your life.

I believe that by taking long periods of rest between every three or four Ironman races, a triathlete can avoid serious injury and burnout and look forward to a long, successful career. Athletes have already proven that it's possible to compete into your fifties and beyond.

(58) SO, YOU DIDN'T FINISH?

So you tried the Ironman and didn't reach that finish line.

First of all, I don't believe there is any such thing as failing in the Ironman.

You most likely went through a lot just to reach the start line and that in itself is quite an accomplishment. Not just anyone is willing to stand on that beach and wait for the starting gun

You probably worked yourself into the best shape of your life just to take your shot at one of the most difficult endurance races in the world. You no doubt earned a lot of respect from those around you who watched as you took up the challenge.

There's lots of reasons why an Ironman race might not work out as you hoped. Possibly you failed to eat and drink properly in that final week. Or maybe you simply overtrained and left your best race out on your favorite bike route back home. If you have even the smallest injury, the Ironman has a way of magnifying it, so it's extremely important that you are 100% going into the race. Possibly you had a nagging injury that carried over into the race.

Some people tend to become very depressed when the race doesn't turn out as they hoped. They go home wondering how they will explain this to everyone who asks them how the Ironman went.

You don't really owe explanations to anyone, but if you must answer, there is one best answer.

"The Ironman is a tough race. That's what makes it special. If it was easy, where would the challenge be?"

Hopefully at that point, you tell that person you intend to try as many times as it takes to reach that finish line.

If anything, not reaching the finish line the first time, or several times you try the race, should be incentive to return until you succeed.

Any race is a learning experience that will help propel you to the finish line the next time.

I had an email from an athlete who had failed five times to reach the finish line and was finally successful in his sixth attempt.

Now to me, he is the true definition of an Ironman.

I can only imagine the huge amount of satisfaction he must feel today.

(59) IRONMAN COEUR D'ALENE

There are many Ironman races now, but I feel it is only right that I talk about the ones I actually experienced in person so I can give first hand information.

Ironman - Coeur d'Alene is one of those courses.

It's the only Ironman that I attempted that was two loops of all three events. Originally, I didn't think I would care too much for it. Especially the swim. I thought it might be a slower time because you actually come out of the water after lap one and run across the beach to begin lap two. Also not being a swimmer, I thought it might be a bit of a let-down to have to get back into the water after reaching shore.

I was completely wrong. I actually had one of my best swim times in Ironman Coeur d'Alene. Also, leaving the water was a bit of a break from the repetitious strokes of the front crawl.

The one thing that sticks out in my mind however, is that the swim start area is quite congested, and things can be a little hairy, especially in the early going. The swim strategy I suggested earlier in the book is ideal for this course. It has been changed to counter-clockwise. In that case, you would be starting on the far right, with the rest of the field and the markers on your left.

The bike course was very interesting and features several down-hill, fast, sweeping curves. Pay attention to the "slow-down" warning signs. There are no "massive" climbs that you'll encounter in Ironman Canada, but plenty of rolling hills and several long, flat stretches. You even make your way though a greyhound race track at one point. The benefit of a 2-loop bike course is that you know exactly what to expect the second time around and are more aware of the challenging high speed turns.

I suppose the most difficult leg to do twice was the marathon. It's really pretty cruel to bring you right past the entrance to the transition area at the end of the first loop. You really have to grit your teeth and push through the turnaround on the marathon course and head back out toward the highway. If I had a choice, I would much rather do an out and back course.

All in all Ironman Coeur d'Alene was an excellent experience. Considering it is quite a new event, the organization was excellent and the volunteers are second to none. Also it's a beautiful, picturesque area for an Ironman and I'm sure you won't go wrong by giving this race a try.

I can see in the near future that Ironman Coeur d'Alene will be a race that will fill quickly and will require very early registration to gain entry.

(60) IRONMAN CANADA

I can tell you quite a bit about Ironman Canada as I've been entered 10 times.

It's very surprising how many choose this particular race for their first Ironman attempt. The reason I say that is because it is very challenging. However, that being said, it is a race with a long history and is a much loved member of the Ironman Triathlon family.

The swim can be really good or really tough. It all depends on the weather and the water temperature. If cooler water is not a problem for you than you should be fine. If it is a problem, the wetsuits you can buy today are quite warm. You can always expect a full complement of around 2000 entries, but the swim start area for this particular race is quite wide. It should not really pose a problem if you have your race plan in place before the big day. This is a single lap course that features two right hand turns.

The bike course requires some restraint. The first 40km or so can be deceiving. Historically this portion is *very* fast. There seems to be a tail wind most years and this part of the course is fairly flat with some long gradual climbs thrown in. The tendency is to go out way too fast. It also gets quite congested in the early going and over the years I've seen many accidents in this stretch. The accidents happen because of the high speeds and the amount of cyclists on this part of the course. It's imperative that you stay to the right and use caution when you pull out to pass. Chances are, there is someone pulling out to pass you as well. Stay away from the center line. Also, don't even think about passing on the right. People have almost ended up in Lake Skaha trying that move.

The reason you don't want to go out too fast in this first 40-45 kms. is because you have Richter's Pass looming just ahead of you. This could well be one of the more difficult climbs in the Ironman race family. I can't say for sure, because I have not done all the other races, but certainly it has to be right near the top of the list. However, there is a reward waiting when you crest the hill and begin the descent. You'll find here that the field is much more spread out now and will remain that way for the rest of the ride.

Some tips about the fast, steep down hills of Ironman Canada:

I talked to a physics professor one year about the difference in accumulated speed between a cyclist who crests a big hill at a very slow speed and one who pedals hard as possible over top and continues doing that until he "spins out" (can't pedal fast enough to keep up with the speed). There is a *huge* difference.

In a nutshell, no matter how tired you are, as you see the top of the hill approaching, stand up and pedal hard over the crest and keep it up as you start down the other side. When you spin out, go into the profile position, and hang on for the ride. The speed you gained at the top will accumulate all the way down and all the cyclists you pass are the ones who relaxed at the crest and let gravity accelerate them.

You might say, "well, I just want to finish the race, so why should I do this?"

It's simple. These are free kilometers and this is free time. You just climbed one of the steepest Ironman hills there is and this is your reward. Build as much speed as you can as you crest the hill, because once you go into the profile position, you are no longer expending energy. This gets you to the finish line that much faster and you must always be aware of the time constraints. Take the free speed where ever you can. Every single year without fail, there are those who miss being official finishers by mere minutes. How much free time did they leave out on the course? Use the same strategy on the Yellow Lake hill. It's kilometer after kilometer of safe, high speed descent. Take full advantage of it. Every kilometer gets you closer to the finish line.

I can't say enough about the Penticton marathon course. For one thing it's out and back. Once you turn at the far end of the course, every step brings you closer to home. The route takes you around Skaha Lake. Much of the lake portion of the run is flat, but there are hills as you get deeper into the run. Again, you work hard to get up those hills. As bad as you may feel, try and take advantage of gravity and run the down hills at any pace you can muster. The marathon is where you will encounter the amazing crowd support and probably some of the top volunteer aid stations in the world. Be sure to acknowledge them. The Penticton Ironman is one of the most established Ironman races and these people are very good at what they do.

Ironman Canada is a fabulous race and people just love it. It fills up in 24 hours. It's almost as hard to get into Ironman Canada as it is to get into Hawaii. I think part of the reason is that it's great to bring the whole family and vacation afterwards.

To get in, you either have to be there the day after the race, or sitting at your computer that Monday first thing and try and get in that way. There are usually enough people just in Penticton to fill the race about half way or more and the rest is done online, and they may possibly have a few lottery spots.

All bets are off however for 2007. There might just be enough people in Penticton at the 2006 edition to fill 2007 completely as Ironman Canada prepares to celebrate its 25th anniversary. The feeling I get, is that many athletes are going out to Penticton just to watch the race and register for 2007.

(61) IRONMAN HAWAII

It's been a long time since I raced in Kona, but I don't believe the Ironman Hawaii course has changed all that much.

The swim course I'm sure, is much the same as it was back in the early 80's. It's truly unforgettable. Water so warm that wetsuits are unnecessary. Tropical fish to marvel at for pretty well the length of the entire course. Water so clear, the bottom is clearly visible. The better to see the scuba divers sitting on the ocean floor, waving at you. The bright orange sails of Captain Bean's boat marking the one and only turn. Its decks overflowing with spectators cheering you on.

Best of all is the current that seems to propel you towards shore as soon as the turn is made. The one downside to the entire swim experience is the sun that will be glaring into your eyes if you breathe to the right on the way back. For this reason alone, I would be sure to be able to breathe comfortably on both sides so you can have at least some relief from the sun if necessary. Also, tinted goggles are a big help. When you can make out the church steeple through the sun's glare, you are almost home and finished the first leg of Iroman Hawaii.

The bike leg for the most part has stayed intact as well. There is no escaping the endless miles of hot asphalt of the now famous King K. highway. The heat made even more oppressive when it's absorbed and reflected by the lava rock that monopolizes the landscape. On the very hot Ironman days, heat waves are clearly visible as you strain to see the road ahead. In 1984 they were our constant companion as the temperature broke through the 100 degree mark out on the highway. To this day Ironman Hawaii 1984 is still the hottest Ironman on record

Then there is the long climb to the turn around that is much more than just another hill. The hot winds sweep in from the ocean and can throw you to the ground in a second if your concentration falters. Finally, on the way home you wait expectantly for the tail winds that are sure to come, but for some reason never materialize.

It's with a great sense of relief and accomplishment that one reaches the bike to run transition only to head back out into nature's oven once again.

The run course thankfully is fairly flat and the climb out of Kona might be the biggest hill of all. I'm not entirely positive as some of the run course has changed. Still once again, there is no avoiding the oppressive heat that has spelled the end to many Ironman dreams, especially for many pros as they are running full out in the heat of the day.

If there is any consolation to being an age grouper intent on just finishing the Hawaii Ironman, it's that you get to run in the coolness that comes with the setting sun.

As you make the turn and head home for the final time it is truly a spectacle to behold as lite-sticks dot the landscape like yellow diamonds flickering in the sudden darkness of the Hawaii night.

The most welcome sight an age grouper can see is the glow from the lights of Kona as you edge closer and closer to one of the most historic endurance race finish lines in the world.

The town is packed with spectators as you reach the long finishing stretch and make the final dash over the same ground that has seen so much drama over the years. Dave Scott, Tinley and the Puntos twins. Mark Allen and Julie Moss. Erin Baker, Paula Newby-Fraser and who can forget Laurie Bowden and husband Peter.

So much history and so many great names. If only it were possible for every Ironman to compete on this hallowed ground. It is just so moving and an experience one can never forget. If you are indeed "Ironstruck," it should be your mission to be part of the grandfather of all Ironman events worldwide.

Ironman Hawaii. So much more than a race.

(62) THE IRONMAN FOREVER

Someone asked me if the Ironman would one day run its course and slowly disappear from the sports landscape.

Personally I would bet that in the early years there were many who watched from the sidelines who believed just that. Especially when anyone who even dared show up at the start line was nothing more than a fit lunatic with a death wish.

When the Ironman was moved to Kona, I'm sure the Iron Gods watched with interest as those adventurous few traveled the shimmering lava fields of the King K. highway. Little did the originators realize that one day they would be recognized as the pioneers of an event that would span the globe and change the lives of anyone with the courage to tame their demons and take up the challenge.

Their strength, courage and unflagging spirit would be the foundation of what has become the most recognized name in endurance sports and not only will it never run its course, it is growing every year and will continue to do so as a new generation picks up the gauntlet and accepts the challenge of the Iron Gods.

Just watch one race and they might just capture you. Glimpse just for a short time an Ironman finish line and you will be seduced by the raw emotion that is laid bare for all to see when someone has given everything they have to give, everything they are, to reach a seemingly unreachable goal. Oh yes, you could indeed be IRONSTRUCK. You could go home and the small seed that is planted will soon take root and your life will take on a new direction.

With every passing day the pull will be stronger and soon like magic, POOF! a new bike will appear. And running shoes. And a wetsuit. And vitamins. And training books. My God! Someone has let the Iron Fairy loose in your home! You will disappear for hours at a time and leave family and friends scratching their heads. "WHERE THE HELL DID SHE GO NOW!"

You will be in bed early and up early. You will become fitter, healthier and will face each day with purpose and will always have one eye on that distant finish line.

You will become a new you. A better you. Pretty amazing since the starting gun is still months away, and the best still to come.

So? Do I think the Ironman will run its course and disappear? I have never been more certain about anything than I am about the longevity of this great event. It is not going anywhere. The Ironman has already been attempted by a family of three generations in the same race. Truly amazing!

For every veteran who parks his tri bike for the last time, there are dozens of the newly "Ironstruck" who have heard the daunting challenge for the first time. The challenge that mystically emanates every time a race unfolds somewhere in the world.

New races continue to spring up in far off corners of the globe. In 2007 China will be host to its first Ironman. Malaysia, the United Kingdom and South Africa are also in the Iron family. Each race generates even more interest and challenges a whole new generation to "show what they are made of."

So, no. The Ironman is not going away. It will be with us for a long, long time.

Just as long as there are those in the world who dare to dream. Those who for the first time have the chance to be so much more. To leave behind, even if for a short time, the constraints of everyday life that in some way has left them unfulfilled. An opportunity perhaps, to reveal the truly amazing individual who has always been just below the surface, waiting for the opportunity to blossom.

The Ironman is that opportunity.

I truly hope that those of you who have read this book find at least one thing that will help you realize your dream. One thing that will inspire you or ease your fear. One thing that will give you the confidence to travel the Ironman highway.

A journey like no other you will ever undertake.

END

To contact the author: http://triathlon-ironman-myfirstironman-ironstruck.com

Printed in Great Britain
by Amazon